Thoughts,
Memories, and
Opinions

Thoughts, Memories, and Opinions

By

Walter Frederick Hammelrath
Commonly known as
Walter Fred Hamelrath

Other Books by Author:

No Arm around My Shoulder

Publisher: Author House

authorHOUSE®

AuthorHouse™ LLC
1663 Liberty Drive
Bloomington, IN 47403
www.authorhouse.com
Phone: 1-800-839-8640

Published by AuthorHouse 07/24/2014

ISBN: 978-1-4969-2662-3 (sc)
ISBN: 978-1-4969-2663-0 (hc)
ISBN: 978-1-4969-2661-6 (e)

Library of Congress Control Number: 2014912650

CONTENTS

PART-I: THOUGHTS

Poems of World War II Years

PART II -MEMORIES

PART III OPINIONS

DEDICATED TO:

My Great-Grandchildren, Kaitlyn, Jonathan, Jackson, Charlie of the Hartzell families and to Daniel and Ryan Brunick my Granddaughter's children. They will grow to adults and never know their Great-Grandfather. This book may help them; later in their lives learn to understand him.

INTRODUCTION

The writings in this book are a potpourri of poems and events that I thought were significant enough to put into words. The initial poems were the result of an English assignment, while a junior in high school. The teacher gave the class an option of writing an essay or a poem. I do not know why I chose the poem, unless I figured it was less work. The result of that choice was a good grade; that opened the door for me to attempt to express my feelings and thoughts in verse. The poems are simple, and do not profess to be of Longfellow or Poe quality. They simply are a way of saying, this is how I felt and thought about the subject, of which I wrote. Some were composed in brief moments of deep thought; others took time to formulate in my mind. Others are an attempt to record, from memory, of a time or an incident that was of significance to me. Not all were set to writing at the time of their occurrence, recorded only when the thought congealed significantly in my mind to write it down. So many good thoughts slipped by retention, never again to be recalled. In my mind, at the moment of conception, they were worthy.

The "Memories" sections are a few of the true events that happened while pursuing a thirty-year career in the US Navy. The "Opinions" section I wrote long after retirement. These opinions reflect on what I have observed happening to our country. Is anyone really watching or listening?

Epilogue

"Ode to Himself"

Acknowledgements

I want to thank Dick Schmidt for his untiring help when I needed assistance with my computer. He was always there, and the calls for help were frequent. Bev Ingersoll, also ever present, to proof read and preview my work. Friends, such as they, contribute immensely to a finished product. My lifetime buddy, Rose Ann, my wife, has always been by my side each step of the way. Her frequent head popping into my bedroom, my study, to see if I was okay and never to say a word of censure as to my long periods of hibernation while writing. All of the above have an unsigned signature to this author's work, without them it probably would not have happened.

PART-I: THOUGHTS

HEALING

Tears form the balm that heals the wounds of the heart.

DECISIONS

I have never regretted any decisions that I have made in my life, be they good ones or bad ones. For from bad decisions came an improvement in Mind and Character, the good ones were rewards in themselves.

A TRIBUTE TO OUR GREAT-GRANDCHILDREN AT CHRISTMAS TIME

Christmas is for children such as you. The beauty of your little faces, the innocence reflected in your lovely eyes, your captivating smile, the tinkle of your voices when you speak, the tenderness of your little hand when it grasps for outreached arms; this is all a continuation of what the Christ Child gave to the world at his birth. You then, are the very meaning of Christmas. May your life always be a carrier of this spirit.

DAY DREAMS

Daydreams are but recesses from the school of daily struggles, which occur in our lives, just a brief respite to rejuvenate the mind.

VANITY AND OLD AGE

When an old rooster loses his vanity, he has nothing left to crow about.

Junior Year in High School\
1939

POEMS

Some of the poems that follow were composed 74 years ago, when I was a young boy filled with fantasies and thoughts of war. Time has faded the original penned writings, but as I read them, the memories come back to life. The period between the end of World War I and the beginning of World War II were formative years for me, and in my simple prose, I set some of my thoughts to verse. In 1940, I enlisted in the Navy and my later compositions reflect my thinking of simple thoughts during those years.

The Land Beyond

There is a beautiful land of somewhere,
Out beyond the blue,
Where everything is peaceful,
And all your dreams come true.

Someday I will sail out there,
When my work on earth is done,
And sit and watch old mother earth,
From my throne up by the sun.

Time Goes On

Time goes swiftly by for me,
In spite of things I do,
Regardless how long I wait,
Or hours I think of you

It seems perhaps its fate,
That leaves me in awhirl,
Or is it high school love,
Because I have met a girl.

I don't know what it is,
Or why I act this way,
But I'll just leave it up to time,
For he'll tell me some day.

Sunset

A splash of color across the sky,
As if paints that had spilled and run,
A splotch of gold, a dash of blue,
Is the setting of the sun.

Rain

The sky turns dark and grumbles,
As if it were filled with pain,
And then the heavens open up,
To send the blessed rain.

Dawn

The morning star begins to fade,
With the breaking of the gloom
And with a rush of sunlight,
The dawn bursts into bloom.

Paradise

Faint and far away
Beside a waterfall
I hear an owl's deep throaty voice
As it sends its evening call.

Across a glen, a deep ravine
Beneath a silvery moon
I hear a coyotes howl afar,
And the whistle of a loon.

Overhead the stars shine down
Upon a world so fair,
And in this paradise I live
Without worry or a care.

Though time will take me from this earth,
No more to walk alone,
I'll still be here in my paradise
My palace and my throne.

A Martyr

In 1865 he died,
A Martyr of fame,
You may not remember him,
Lincoln was his name.

A pistol shot snuffed out his life,
This man of hope's bright ray,
And though he lived in year's gone bye
His soul still lives today.

The Duck's Flight

In columns straight they come head on,
Like Army fighting planes,
They battle wind, snow and sleet,
Lightning and the rain.

Their colored bodies glisten,
As they pass us overhead,
They are not filled with sorrow,
Nor are they filled with dread.

They know just what to do,
When they hear the leader's call,
For they are flying south you see,
They do this every fall.

They Fought For Us

They fought a war to end all wars,
To make this old world free,
To do away with Lords and Kings,
To restore Democracy.

They gave their lives so we could live,
Like humans ought to do,

They died in France not for themselves,
But for me and others too.

Call of the North

Far, far away o'er mountains high,
Beyond the cities far,
I long to go and live alone,
Beneath the northern star.

I want to get away from here,
And roam among the pines,
For my soul is filled with longing,
For those far off northern signs.

I dream of the river Yukon,
And the trails of ice and snow,
I feel the call of the far off North,
And a voice inside, says go.

A Soldier's Soul Speaks

My life was taken from me,
In the battle of the Marne,
A seventy-seven blew me to bits,
As we stormed a farmer's barn.

I felt no pain, just one quick flash,
Then silence cold and dread,
And I walked into a land of light,
The barracks of the dead.

All is quiet and peaceful here,
No sound of cannons roar,
No rattle of the rifle fire,
No more the horror of war.

Never again to hear the cry,
"Of charge and Fire at Will"
Never again to take a life,
Or human blood to spill.

I have done my part to make world peace,
To help "Old Glory Fly"
And my sole reward was death,
So in "Flanders Field" I lie.

Air Raid

Swooping low over cities
Their missiles of death they drop,
And with each loud explosion
The race of life is stopped.

Wings against the darkened sky,
Searchlights stab the night,
Screams of pain of the dying,
Useless in their plight.

Sirens scream and people run,
To save themselves if they can,
Gone are their thoughts of culture,
And the ways of civilized man.

A Mother's Prayer for Her Son

Dear Lord I dreamed I saw him,
A skeleton grim and gaunt,
Lying on the battle field,
His face my thoughts to haunt.

I dread to think of such a thing,
But yet I feel it so,

7

Please, Oh Lord, take care of him,
Wherever he may go.

He was only seventeen, My Lord,
When he sailed for war in France,
So young, so strong, so very gay,
So full of innocence.

This prayer I give to thee,
My blessings with it go,
I will trust in thee, Oh Lord,
I know you will make it so.

The Unknown Soldier Speaks

I am the "Unknown Soldier"
In Arlington Cemetery I lie,
Unknown to thousands of people,
Who yearly pass me bye.

Unknown to many a mother,
Whose son was killed in war,
Unknown to nations of people,
These and a thousand more.

My life is filled with glory,
When my tomb they decorate,
But I would rather lie in Flanders Field
With a cross to decorate.

To World War I Veterans

He was standing there in the doorway,
As I hurriedly passed him by,
An overseas cap was on his head,
And his collar was turned up high.

He seemed to be staring into space,
Not knowing what to do,
So I doffed my hat and softly said,
"Can I do anything for you?"

He smiled at me and answered,
"No sonny, no one wants me,
You see I fought in the last World War,
In France across the sea.

They don't want any veterans around,
To work for them today,
They say, we are old and helpless and
Only in the way."

As he spoke these words, his eyes grew dim,
And a tear rolled down his face,
And I thought of the thousands of other men,
Who through our hands had met disgrace.

Our Chaplain

He lifts me to enlightened heights
From depths of dark despair,
He makes the world seem right again
Free from toil and care.
He gives a word of courage
In time of need or pain,
This man is our good Chaplain,
A server in God's Domain

Farewell

Goodbye to the good old USA
We sail tomorrow morning
For the battle fields in France,
Where troops are daily swarming.

Goodbye to home and friends so dear,
Where flowers this spring are bright,
We are sailing away from here
To where bombs and flares are light.

So long mother, dad and sis,
I know I will never return,
But please be brave for just my sake,
And let the lamplight burn.

Navy Enlistment Pledge

We took a pledge,
Only words to us then,
But since has changed us
From boys to men.

Though many shall die
In the ocean deep,
This pledge of allegiance
We will always keep.

Taps

Through the camp
Its notes rolled clear
As the dusk of eve drew nigh,
Like a beautiful hymn
Or a prayer,
Like an infant's loving sigh.

No call, no order not even a shout
This silent message
In even laps
Drifts o'er the lake,
As the bugle sounds taps.

My Son

There is an empty spot in my heart tonight,
There is a vacant chair by my side,
And in my eyes, there is a trace of a tear,
For my son who sails with the tide.

Often in visions, I see him alone,
When at eve by my bedside I pray
For that far off time when he shall return
To his home forever to stay.

But in the end if he should die
From the shell of an enemy gun,
I will dry that tear and softly smile,
For he would want it that way, my son.

I'm "Gonna" Be Good

I am gonna be a good boy,
And help my mom and dad,
I'm gonna do everything I can
To make them feel so glad.

I'll carry out the ashes,
And fill the wood box too,
I'm gonna do a lot of things,
"Cause there are heaps of things to do.

I'll run errands for my mom,
And help her with the dishes,
And I'll be real nice to her,
And wish her best of wishes.

Yes sir, I'll be a nice little boy
I'll do no wrong don't you fear,
'Cause gosh all fish hooks can't you see
That Christmas is almost here.

11

POEMS OF WORLD WAR II YEARS

Awakening

When dawn's early curtain rises,
Across the stage of the world,
And Apollo rears his head forth,
Then another day is unfurled.

When the dewdrops fade,
And the grass and flowers
Awaken from slumber
From the long night hours.

When the cock in the barnyard
Crows loud and long,
Then I awaken with joy
To this morning song.

Years

Through tear dimmed eyes
I gaze at the past,
Years of hardships
Are finished at last.

Years of sorrows,
Years of joys,
Years that mold us
Like simple toys.

Life is like that
From beginning to end,
The years of our life
Is the price we spend.

What a Buddy Means to Me

Now I just met a buddy,
A kid from my own hometown.
And when I saw his smiling face,
I lost my worried frown.

For somehow in our meeting,
I recalled when just we two,
Were just young lads of mischief.
Doing things that kids shouldn't do.

Sure, his smile brought back the memories,
It wiped my dark clouds clear

And left me quite contented
To know a friend was near.

It is strange in all my travels,
In all the curious things I see,
That there is never a more joyous moment,
Than when an old friend speaks to me.

We talked, I guess an hour or more,
Of things which marked our goal,
And I in lonely passion,
Emptied out my wearied soul.

For there's nothing like a buddy,
When the mind is all unrest,
He seems to have a hidden power
Which calms ones thoughts to rest.

News Item

Four flags stood out on her bridge
She reeked of death they said,
Of powder stains and blasted steel.
And blood where the wounded bled.

Her guns were warped and blackened,
The forward boilers dead,
A gaping hole yawned in her side,
Like a monsters ugly head.

She took that "fish" and a strafing,
Gave them back a helluva blow
To earn those flags on the bridge,
The flags of the beaten foe.

At her rail her crew stood proudly,
What was left of her rank and file,

And on every battle worn face
There was a confident champion's smile.

The name of the ship I can't give you,
The censor's banned her name,
But she stands for glory and freedom,
And she is manned by men of fame.

Real Heroes

On Guadalcanal the palm trees grow,
Burned and blasted row on row.
They mark the graves of brave Marines,
Who bled and died with hideous screams.

On this lonely isle so far remote
Their blackened bodies rot and bloat,
And day by day, their ranks decrease,
Self sacrificed for one word "Peace".

Lest we forget when this war is done,
All papers signed, and we have won,
That on this lonely isle, true heroes will stay,
Twisted in death as they feel that day,
While through the palms a soft breeze blows,
Whispering a prayer for those silent rows.

The Lad in Navy Blue

Say girlie, I saw you sneer just then,
Don't I look good enough for you,
I am not quite in your class, Huh.
For wearing this Navy Blue.

You think I am not fine enough
For such a girl as you.

15

Well! There are men who would not hold your hand
Who have worn the Navy Blue.

You ban us from your family home
And from your ballrooms too.
There is room for all,
Except the lad in Navy Blue.

We are only common sailors,
"Till war's hell starts to brew,
And then my dear your start to cheer
For the lads In Navy Blue.

I know that I am not a fashion plate,
That's not my style it's true,
But, listen closely dear,
It takes a man, to wear the Navy Blue.

So when I am done and gone
And life's last cruise is through,
I will not be barred from Heaven
For wearing the Navy Blue.

Curse of the Deep

At the change of the tide, I'll take her in
With a fair blowing breeze from astern,
I'll berth her tight and secure there
'Till there's no more money to burn.

When I've had me first drink of raw whiskey,
Knocked the sea dust from my veins,
I'll anchor my hull in some sinkhole of sin,
And secure me some sea-faring Jane.

I've got a sea story to tell them,
Of endless days on the blue,

Where wind and rain beating madly
Can strip all the saneness from you.

You curse your shipmates you hate them,
You damn the tropical heat
That grinds you down or breaks you,
And you feel in your soul that you're beat.

You long for the love of a woman,
Your passion is your only desire,
It burns like liquor, on an open wound,
And it tortures your soul with its fire.

There are girls in those tropical hellholes,
Fat, big breasted, just sluts,
You dream for a girl of fair beauty,
This other kind tortures your guts.

There are only two things that you live for,
A woman with skin white as snow,
A barrel of gut burning whiskey,
Which in wonder never ceases to flow.

At times, you awaken screaming
From the deep oblivion of sleep,
Tormented by ghostly nightmares,
Of the horrors, you have seen on the deep.

The daylight is hated, unwelcome,
They say because of the heat,
So you dwell in the shadows of nightfall and hope,
That it covers all sinners retreat.

Beautiful stars above lose their romance,
Though through the rigging they still shine as jewels,
Airy clouds borne lightly as zephyrs
Are just clouds to those lifeless fools.

It's a life not suited for many,
Only those who are strong minded men.
It rips you apart a thousand times,
Then knocks you together again.

You feel you are slipping, with the passing of time,
The cruises out each time seem worse,
And you damn the bloody bastard to hell
Who gave you this sea-going curse.

Still when all of your money has vanished
To the pockets of whores or in bars,
You'll still sign on again,
And sail with the wind and the stars.

Craftsman "God"

Have you ever watched a mason
As he builds a high brick wall?
The skill he applies in making it
So when finished it ne'er shall fall.

Have you ever watched a painter
As he paints a flock of sheep,
Or a picture of the "Virgin Mary"
And the "Christ Child" fast asleep?

Have you ever thought of the Craftsman
Who molded the grass and flowers,
Or who made the seconds and minutes
That make the endless hours,

Or who made the mighty mountains,
The streams, and lakes and sod.
He is the world's most skillful Craftsman,
To us he is known as "God".

Epitaph

God Bless the crew of the Reuben James
May their souls rest in peace,
And may the praises of these brave men
Live on never to cease.

To their loved ones give a medal,
In public squares, erect a plaque,
For that is the least we can give them,
These lads who never came back.

Let this be an inspiration
To the rest of the men in the fleet,
We will avenge these lads of the Reuben James,
Who never knew defeat.

When this task of ours is over,
When the muster is read and done,
We will shout our praise to the Lord above,
For them we have fought and won.

The Past

When the sun has set o'er the river,
And the shadows have lengthened and gone,
When the stars have appeared like jewels overhead,
And the nightingale has warbled his song.

Then I sit alone on my doorstep
Thinking of days long past.
Those days of my boyhood, how happy they were,
Long gone and ever so fast.

I hold no hopes of the future,
The joys of existence are dead.
I only live in the past of my life,
For the future is all vague and dread.

19

When War Clouds Fade

When the winds of peace shall blow again,
And the war clouds fade away,
When the "Rising Sun" has set,
And the "Swastikas" have had their day.

When the sun shines rays of glory
On the peaceful scenes below,
And each neighbor wears a smile
As he wanders to and fro.

When an infant's wailing cry
Means a new life, not one lost,
When a blackout is just a legend,
And the coldest hates defrost.

In my mind, that is our future,
Our ambitions and desires.
Let us strive to reach that goal
Lest it die from War Lords fires.

A Sailor's Thoughts

A heaving deck beneath you,
A clear blue sky above,
The call of the sea within you,
And the clash of the waves you love.

The feel of the wheel before you,
As the bow bites deep in the sea,
The lookouts call, "Land Ho" me lads,
Yes, that is the life for me.

A dash of spray upon your cheek,
A cannons roar at your side,
The well-known clank of the anchor chain,
As you come to rest with the tide.

Then silence falls about you,
Your thoughts fade from the sea,
You are left in your drab surroundings,
The rest just a memory.

Hobo's Song

The whistle blows far up ahead
Its shrill notes echo back,
As I roll along in my box car home,
With a clackity, clackity, clack.

I have no cares or sorrows,
No troubles or remorse,
For they are whisked away with the clackity, clack
That comes from my old iron horse.

I love the smell of the engines smoke,
The speed of a fast down grade,
And the vibrant tune of clackity, clack
As she roars on unafraid.

Through the inky blackness of the night,
By city and whistle stop.
That clackity, clack carries me on
To tomorrow and the top.

The top of the world and freedom,
For I am a hobo of the trail,
And the clackity, clack is my marching song,
My band is the singing rail.

Advice to a Son

Son of mine, today you leave

To pit your knowledge against a world war torn,
A world blood crazed, unfamiliar, time worn.
Temptations you'll find at every turn.
Friends you'll find, but some you'll spurn

Plant both feet on the road of right and trust
In God alone, this you must.
For strange as ways and customs are today
The light of God still leads the way.

This is all I have to offer as I am bent with years,
Just the knowledge of hardships that were earned by many tears.
Go son, God bless you, may your successes be great,
Remember opportunity knocks but once, and time will never wait.

The Gob with the Swab

Now you have heard of the poem "The Man with the Hoe",
And the man with the shovel I am sure,
But the Gob with the swab has never been versed,
So a few rhyming lines I'll conjure.

He's the barefooted lad on the poop deck,
Or the lumbering hick by the rail,
But wherever he goes soap and water flows,
Its source, his swab and his pail.

The "Knight" of the deck force his title,
His swab he twirls as a lance,
His uniform strange, this lad from the range,
Wears naught but a pair of old pants.

He slinks through the dark of the dawning,
The hour before six, I am told,
Through foul weather or shine, this hero of mine
Swabs on like sea dogs of old.

On tin cans and cruisers, you'll find him,
In fact, all ships of the fleet,
And in spite of his rate, seaman or mate
He keeps our ships looking neat.

"The Man with the Hoe" earned dollars galore,
Three hundred thousand, I think,
But the "Gob with the Swab" in spite of his job,
Ain't even earned a free drink.

No Dice at Love

At chuck-a-luck or faro,
In poker games or dice,
I have always won the greenbacks,
And my bankbook is looking nice.

Roulette I love, and black jack
Send shivers up my spine,
When the dealer hollers "Win Again",
Then Lady Luck is mine.

I have played the ponies also,
I take the biggest odds,
My horses always come in first,
They lead the field by rods.

Yet romance is my pitfall,
I have bet on all the field,
Blondes, brunette or redhead,
My winnings still don't yield.

I have tried them with a cold deck
Of flowers, champagne and such,
But they always slip me two small pair,
In love, I lack the touch.

So to hell with all of your women,
I give cupid the old bums rush,
I will stick to the gambling tables every time,
For you can't beat an old "Royal Flush".

Our Hero

To the unsung man of the Navy,
The pride of all the Fleet.
The lad who stokes the boilers,
Through grease, and grime and heat.

To the man deep down in the bilges,
Who seldom sees light of day,
Who answers the bridges signals,
That keeps the ship underway.

To the lad who cleans the firesides,
Just one of a million tasks.
Just let him sleep to seven o'clock,
That is all he really asks.

When all the deck hands slumber,
He works on down below
To feed the oil to the boilers,
Should the steam gage get to low.

You ask me who this lad is,
And why I drink this toast.
Is he so bright and noble?
That all of us should boast.

My answer is a short one,
Yes, he is God's own right-hand man.
He is the ship's own unsung hero,
He is the lowly fireman.

Shifting Sand in My Shoes

Shifting sand in my shoes
Is like the wanderlust call,
That keeps driving me onward,
Rolling, hitting the ball.

Like a beacon it beckons,
Makes me get up and git,
For I have no home to leave from,
'Cause my homes where I sit.

It is that call of the desert,
Or that cry from the sea
That sets my feet wandering,
And won't let me be.

The torch of the ages
That made man pioneer,
To the land we now live in
Under blue skies so clear.

It knows no bounds or restrictions,
It calls when it may,
And I answer in reverence,
For I know I can't stay.

The blood of my life,
Its pulse beat I can't abuse,
I can only answer its call,
Shifting sand in my shoes.

Rendezvous

Twilight and evening shadows
Across the blue lagoon,
Where nightingales are calling
To the lazy summer moon.

25

Crickets' creek and chirp
Down by the water's edge,
And shadows play in rhythm
To the wind along the hedge.

Two lovers meet
And hand in hand
They walk in silence
Along the sand.

In their rendezvous
Alone they meet,
A haven of rest
In nature's retreat.

Life

Life is like a book, each day corresponds to one page. Each page added to another, with all of its comments and happenings forms a chapter, which in a man's life may constitute a year, a month or even a decade.

The book of life has its theme, although at times we find it hard to uncover. It has its setting, climax and ending. There is tragedy, comedy, and even a little fantasy or melodrama on the side. Each of these helps build the book from just a story to a novel.

The greatest novel ever written, that of life. To my knowledge, no finer plot has ever been written. Thus when the book is finished it means another soul has passed away, but there still remains the "Book of Life" of their adventures, sorrows and joys to freshen our minds of their once presence here on earth.

My Idaho

Between the blue of the ocean,
And the Rockies covered with snow,
Lies a bit of nature's heaven,
I call it "My Idaho".

God's gift to us simple people,
Is the fertile sod and streams,
Where we live in sweet contentment,
Idaho, land of my dreams.

Where fish and game are abundant,
Blue sky and sun every day,
Tall pines to the north behind us,
Sweep down to the desert to play.

Dark nights with stars like rubies,
And the coyotes howling below,
To the wisps of clouds and the moonlight,
That's home, "My Idaho".

If on foreign soil, they shall lay me,
In my heart I will always know,
That really I'll always be buried,
Back there in "My Idaho".

The Idaho Bumble Bee

In all of my life long travels
I have yet to see,
A meaner or ornerier critter
Than the Idaho Bumble Bee.

He has a foot long stinger,
And he uses it you can bet.
He's has the darndest habit
Of putting it where you set.

27

You'll find him at all the picnics,
On Sunday auto drives,
He comes to every shindig,
And he brings his whole damn hive.

He eats our jams and jellies,
Then stings our babies too,
And when you try to swat him
He pours the rod to you.

So come on all you big game hunters,
Who long for some decree,
Add a new one to your string,
The "Idaho Bumble Bee".

Today I am Blue

Today I am blue and lonely,
For the skies above are grey,
And raindrops splashing against the glass,
In unison, seem to say.

Oh! For those happy days of youth,
When I was young and gay,
When the trivial things of life were great,
And you lived with joy each hour of the day.

As a lad you trooped and romped
From morn till dark across the meadows so serene,
And knew and loved each flower and bird,
That grew in the forest green.

You yet recall each eventide,
When you sat with rapturous joy,
Beside your grandfather's rocking chair,
While he told of his days as a boy.

And how you wished that you were he,
And could have lived those hell roaring days,
And shot it out with a bandit bold,
To prove that crime never pays.

Yes, today I am blue and lonely,
For the skies are dark and cold,
But most of all I am lonely,
Because I have lived, and now I am old.

Dear Friend

The following poem was written, and sent to, Florence M. Rees, my surrogate family member, during the early part of World War II. Miss Rees, "Pete", as she liked to be called, was the dearest friend I had as a lad of 17 and 18. She was my Speech and Drama teacher, who taught me more than any instructor I have ever had. Many were the times I poured out my soul to her, when problems at home were tearing me apart. She would always sit and listen to my tearful out-pouring of my problems. She was my confident friend, always there when I needed a friendly shoulder to lean on. My most painful regret is I never managed to keep in touch with her after the war years, as I continued my career in the navy. Beyond this poem, I never told her how much I loved her as a person, and as a teacher of the highest order. Wherever she may be, may this remembrance reach her.

You Were Always There

Today I got your letter,
I knew you still were there,
Backing every move, I made,
Helping to do your share.

When I read those lines, you wrote
About how special I was to you,
I could only smile and swallow,
Because I think the same of you.

29

When I got the "willies"
You called them sentimental blues,
I always looked to you for help,
For there I found my cues.

You told me always I was right,
Never did you reprimand,
Just serve your God and country,
By your side I'll always stand.

Sure, you helped me build my future,
Watch it shape and disappear,
When I enlisted in the Navy
You said it is better than staying here.

Now I know just why you said that,
My place is with the right.
You taught me everything I know,
Just forget, get in and fight.

You always like that side of me,
That used to whoop and holler,
About my political thinking,
Or how daily we waste our dollars.

But that is just why I love you,
With your knowing eyes that care,
For when I needed someone,
I just turned and you were there.

Getting No Place
I dream of home and good cigars,
Of whiskey, girls, and rowdy bars,
Of salty tales of battle scars,
But here I sit, getting no place.

I yell and yap and beat my gums,
I cuss the shore based V-6 bums,
They get the breaks the dirty scums,
But here I sit, getting no place.

The transfers come; the transfers go,
I sweat them all I guess you know,
I'm just a sailing G.I. Joe,
But here I sit, getting no place.

I bang my ears just like the rest,
I'm just a typical wardroom pest,
And I'll have you know I'm one of the best,
But here I sit, getting no place.

My cabbage is growing on the books,
Why I can soon hire me valets and cooks,
And have a blonde for just good looks,
But here I sit, getting no place.

So when they yell its "Armistice Day"
They will transfer me to the beach to stay,
And I'll weep and moan as they sail away,
"Cause here I sit, going no place.

Woodland Knights

The woodland knights have laid away their armor
Bared brown and wrinkled bodies to the winds
Which cuts among their stalwart ranks
And beats against their rugged limbs.

The Spanish moss, with banners bright
That used to hang from arms out-flung,
Now has withered, died, and turned to dust
Like heroes dead, unheard, unsung.

31

Where once below on carpets green,
That now in somber colors lay,
They stood as guardians of the land
To watch the old and young at play.

Lifeblood that flowed so strong in youth,
And gave these knights pure hearts of fire,
Now flows like sluggish currents of lead,
The winter blasts suggest, retreat, retire,

Like shaggy bears they hibernate,
They sleep for short months known to all,
Then with the first faint signs of spring,
They stretch and yawn to duties call.

Upon those withered bodies brown,
New life and armor springs with ease,
The woodland knights take hold again,
Flower forth in glory, splendid trees.

It had been 15 days since the Japanese Forces had attacked Pearl Harbor Hawaii. The water was still covered with fuel oil from the sunken ships. The many fires had been extinguished, and the USS Tangier AV8, my ship, had received new orders. Wake Island, further to the west in the Pacific, was under attack and badly in need of reinforcements. Task Force 14 had been established and Tangier, because of her capability to carry a large amount of troops and supplies, had been assigned to this Task Force, which consisted of the Aircraft Carrier USS Saratoga, three cruisers, nine destroyers, an oiler and the Tangier. On the 15 December 1941, Tangier got under way to join this group. This would be the first sortie of naval forces since the attack. The arrival date at Wake Island was to be 23 December; this never happened as the Japanese over took the island. The Tangier, with two destroyers as escorts, was diverted to Midway Island.

The following poem I composed one night while on watch in the engine room, while enroute to Wake Island. I wrote it to the tune of "The Wabash Cannonball", and it became the song that the crew would always remember at the reunions we had after the war. The ship had performed well during the attack, shooting down three planes, and possibly a couple more. The words convey how a very frightened young engine room fireman thought of his ship.

Tangier Song
(Tune: Wabash Cannonball)

Her keel was laid in Frisco
She's a freighter by her birth
Her decks are made of scrap iron
So I don't know what she's worth,

But her lines they are graceful
And her masts they are so tall
She's a seagoing combination
Of the Wabash Cannonball.

From Frisco to Shanghai
She plows the briny deep,
She's the watchdog of the Navy
That guards you while you sleep.

She's master of the ocean
She's the scourge of all the sea,
She's Uncle Sammy's freighter,
The Navy's terrible "T:

East and West, and North and South
We're known both far and near,
We travel by the moniker
Of the USS Tangier.

Our crew is trusty buckos,
A tougher lot you ne'er did see
Than the shoot' in', fight' in'
Dynamiting' crew of the terrible "T.

She can be a seaplane tender
Or a battlewagon strong,
She can be an inspiration
To a lonesome sailor's song.

She has carried us to foreign ports
In lands across the foam,
Let us pray to God, she stays afloat,
So she can take us home.

USS Tangier AV 8

A new C-3 was the terrible "T"
When the Navy took her over,
With a lot of sweat and a little paint
She became a good sea rover.

They fitted her out with the best damned
Crew that ever paced a deck,
Then gave her a couple of VP Squadrons to nurse,
The usual pain in the neck.

She was christened with fire at Pearl Harbor,
She stood her post like a Queen,
And when the smoke of battle cleared
Her colors could still be seen.

In New Caledonia, she made a home
For soldiers and gobs alike.
She gave her best in every job
From Noumea to the Pike

Now once again at this lonely isle,
Called Esperito Santos
She lays and waits for the wily "Jap"
To come and get a dose.

But if some day she should sink
Beneath the white capped wave,
Her spirit still will sail ever on,
Should her hull find a watery grave.

If It Could Only Be

As I stood on the threshold of the future
I dreamed of things to come,
Of a world free from greed and hate,
And a life of love and fun.

I foresaw a modern Utopia,
A long dreamed of Shangri La,
Through the golden gates of the future,
These are the things I saw.

There cradled in the heart of a valley
Lay a city by a cold mountain stream,
A beauteous piece of construction,
Built of air castles and dreams.

The sky that covered this Eden
No clouds of expression or might,
Just a simple but happy life,
One of reverence and right.

Then soft as a dead leaf falling
The masterful "present" took my hand,
And I returned to earthly hell once more,
Just a dreamer of that wonderful land.

Shadows and Life
When darkness falls across the land,
Like the gentle touch of a woman's hand,
Soft and light, its shadows mingle,
Yet it seems to knowingly single
One lone soul, which is laid to rest,
And in that soul, we see the best,
For good things far outshine the bad,
And happiness dispels the sad
Shadows will stay as long as they can,
Thus in their image they symbolize man.

Faithfully They Wait
His hunting coat hangs in the hallway,
Nearby stands his favorite gun,
On the floor lay his mud-caked boots,
As he left them, when he last returned from the run.

And soulfully crouching by
With their eyes on his hunting gear,
The hound dogs he loved wait patiently
For the call of his voice so clear.

They seem to know he's gone,
It tells in their deep brown eyes,
But faithfully still they wait for him,
Anxious to hear his cries.

For now he hunts on larger fields,
He stalks a bigger game,
He has given himself to his country
To help preserve Democracy's name

Though he may be gone forever,
And his gear in the hallway rusts,

His hound dogs still wait faithfully,
Though his bones may have turned to dust.

Lonesome Pine

A lonesome sentinel the old pine stands
Up, on the mountain high,
Twisted, gnarled, and bent with age,
Clutching for the sky.

Roots that grasp for moisture,
Weak yet holding fast,
Striving for bare existence,
On this barren peak so vast.

Suffering from the elements of
Nature's unleashed wrath,
Staunch old sentinel
Guarding each beaten path.

Though withered and scarred from weather
It's somehow majestically divine,
A symbol of strength and solitude,
This old wind warped lonesome pine.

Sundown

When it's sundown on the desert
Then it's twilight 'round half the world,
As that golden orb the sun sinks behind the hill,
There the spectrum tinted fingers of
The sunset interlace with the
Purple shadows of the mountains and the moor.
For a few brief flitting seconds
They lock in mortal struggle, then
The Shadows of the evening from the daylight takes its place.
It's the time when the million little

37

People; put their troubles of the day behind them
And partake of nature's beauty here at hand.
For at sundown cares are forgotten,
Sad and lonely hearts enlightened
As the evening shadows cast their mystic spell.
Then without a moments warning
The darkness steals upon us,
And the splendor of the sunset is no more.
But we know that on the morrow
With its troubles and its sorrows
Once again the banners of the sunset will be unfurled,
And as God had intended the soul of man
Will be contented and it will be
Sundown again 'round half the world.

Eventide

The last golden rays of sunlight
Filtered down through the trees,
And old magnolias sigh softly
With the heavily perfumed breeze.

Up the cow path from the creek
The cows in single file,
Wobble slowly homeward
Content for just this while.

All around you hushed and silent,
Yet somehow, so beautifully serene,
The woodlands, farms, and life itself
Seem somehow like a dream.

The shadows slipping like some ghost
From tree to tree and round,
Mystically, quietly, awe-inspiring,
Yet uttering no sound.

With this all about you,
Friend nature by your side,
At dusk each day I give you
God's beauty, eventide.

The South Sea Calls

Overhead the white sails billow,
Behind trails the phosphorous sea,
And on the breeze that blows from the south
The South Sea calls to me.

Tall palms lie before me,
White beaches of volcanic isles,
While up above the clear blue sky
Is filled with white cloud piles.

Long nights with the smell of wild flowers
Drifting down on an island breeze,
With the big full moon away up there
Shining down through the banyan trees,

Weird songs of the singing natives,
And throbbing drums of the tribal rites,
These many things come back to me,
On the wind of the South Sea nights.

Adventure lies before me,
It beckons with outstretched hand,
So I will sail with the tide in the morning,
To the call of the South Sea land.

If Time Had Permitted

A pirate bold I want to be,
To sack and plunder on the sea,

With skull and cross bones atop my mast,
On land and sea my vengeance cast
With the clash of steel ringing in my ear,
And the boom of the surf none I fear.
My course the seven seas I ply,
Sails blocked by wind, stars and sky.
To drop anchor in harbors clear,
Sweep the decks with a broadside of a privateer,
Pieces of eight from the Spanish Main
Upon my crew I would freely rain.
While silks and satins I would wear,
Taken from the king with greatest care.
My trail of blood would scar the earth,
In muffled tones men would curse my birth
To die, perhaps, from a yardarm high,
Silhouetted clearly against the sky,
With roll of drum and shrill of fife,
Thus I would live, for that is life.
But alas, time alone was my fate,
For I was born two hundred years too late.

The Golden Gate

To those of you who have never seen
The Golden Gate from the seaward side,
As you come drifting home again
To anchor with the tide.

Then you have missed a wondrous sight,
Which warms a sailor's heart,
The glow of city lights at night
From which you've been apart.

A golden moon, which hangs above,
That gave the Golden Gate its name,
The peaceful star winking back

To those seekers of fortune and fame

That evening breeze which softly blows
Across the limpid bay
Carries all the scents of home,
And beckons you to stay.

Ferryboats go chugging past,
As you come drifting in
With all the people there on deck,
Seeming to ask where you've been.

Then underneath that monstrous span,
Which spreads across the bay,
You pass into this paradise,
Forever, you hope, to stay.

My Conscience

He's a funny person,
In spite of himself,
He's here and there
Like a storybook elf.

He makes me laugh,
When I feel mad,
And when I'm happy
He makes me sad.

He's my conscience,
My minds his home,
His highways my thoughts
On which to roam.

And though he's mean
As mean, as mean can be,
We'll never part

'Cause my conscience is me.

Dreamland

Come take my hand my darling,
Let's climb the "Milky Way",
That bridges earth with heaven,
When night has conquered day.

We'll sit and dream in wonderland,
Amid the stars and moon,
Upon the velvet spread of night
That passes far too soon.

I'll pluck a jewel for you my dear,
A star as it passes by,
A crown I'll place upon your head,
My princess of the sky.

We'll wile away the languid hours
High above the chimney tops,
Perhaps we'll share a dream of two,
And pray that time would stop.

But on the far horizon dim,
Dawns the light of day,
So we must clamber down again,
And leave our realm the "Milky Way".

Live To Fulfillment

Oh! Why so blindly through this life
Do humans ply their way,
Never living to fulfillment
God's enraptured, beauteous day.

Never seeking out the whys or wherefores,

Just content to daily live.
Oh! Such fools that toss aside
All the teachings God did give.

Think they not of such small instants
Like the sunset or the dawn,
Seeing yes, but not observing,
These ungrateful, devil's spawn.

Not one second do they tarry,
Stop to cherish for a while,
Green and fertile farms or hillsides,
Kissed and blessed by nature's smile

Curse these blind and careless people,
Through their eyes they cannot see
All the magnificence of God's Kingdom,
They're the ones that ought not be.

For to live, and live each moment
That is filled with joy so gay,
Will reward thee with fond memories,
When all else has passed away.

The End of the Schooner "Bat"

It was one of those days in November,
When the leaves were beginning to fall,
That we left for Nova Scotia
Fighting a nasty squall.

The wind tore at the rigging,
Its wailing pierced the night,
We pitched and tossed on the ocean's crest
Like a dancing candle's light.

With main sail reefed. and mizzen furled,
We plowed on through the dark,

43

With little thought on our minds
That we would lose our bark.

We hit the reef a head on blow,
Our hull was caved in flat,
And with a sigh of the moaning wind,
There sank the schooner "Bat".

No one lived but me,
To tell of the ghastly tale,
Of the turmoil that followed
Through the crashing of the gale.

Often in my sleep, I see her,
Now sailing on a sea so flat,
Riding calm on the ocean's crest,
The bonny schooner "Bat".

Forest Wonderland

As the first gray shadows of evening fall,
I hurry to my forest wonderland,
Where 'mid the cypress dripping wet,
All veiled with Spanish Moss, alone I stand.

Long streamers of wraith like fog
Come drifting silently by,
Like specters of another world,
And you startle at a curlew's cry.

Here light of day is seldom bright,
And shadows oft' betray the mind,
You see that which are not there,
Only silhouettes well defined.

Thus with the night falling 'round me,
More fantasies add to my dream,

Fireflies lighting up this world
Ruled by some Fairy Queen.

Rustlings in the underbrush,
Perhaps a dwarf or two,
And then the frightened eyes of a chipmunk
Stare curiously back at you.

All night I watch these creatures,
Who work or play while we sleep,
Remote from all humanity
In the heart of the forest deep.

At last the cold gray dawn breaks,
I leave my forest of dreams,
For the light of day spoils everything,
And my wonderland is not what it seems.

A Letter to Davy Jones

Now Davy old boy just save me a place
In your realm down under the sea,
For any old time I will likely breeze in
With the rest of the crew from the "T"

So save me a bunk and a locker,
My space keep shipshape and clear,
For I'm traveling heavy this cruise out
I have a hell of a lot of gear.

A table for two at the "Rusty Hull"
I'd certainly like if you would manage,
Don't spare the trimmings, Davy old boy,
For I'll be packing plenty of cabbage.

You'd better round up all the femmes for me,
The best that your realm can provide,

45

For I change my women as often old man
As there is a change of the tide.

Make out an order for whiskey too,
No rot gut, for I drink the best.
I know there's plenty of stuff down there,
Stowed away in your old sea chest.

If you've no blue serge for a suit of blues,
Get hot I want the best you can get,
For after I have traveled from here to there
Mine's likely to be ruined and wet.

Put in an ad for a cozy shack,
So my women can live with an ease,
For I like my privacy most of all,
When I'm loving and batting the breeze.

Make sure the sack is soft and dry,
And wide enough for two,
For I'm planning on making some broads down there,
That would even be shocking to you.

Now I guess that's all, so let's get hot,
Things topside might not last as I planned,
And if they don't I want things ready,
So I can start as soon as I land.

Those Shipping Over Blues

Oh! How well my memories linger on
Of that day some years ago,
When I got my walking papers,
My first cruise over you know.

How proud I stood on the Quarter Deck,
My sea bag packed with my gear,

And deep in its own little corner
Lay my discharge I cherished so dear.

Oh! The smile that wrinkled my ugly pan,
When I thought of the guys left behind,
Who had snowed me for hours on Navy bull
Of the life I would get if I signed.

As I slung up my gear to my shoulder,
My lips formed these words to say,
"May I have permission to leave the ship"
When loud blares the song Anchors Aweigh.

My lips closed on soundless words,
Before my eyes formed the past,
And damned if I didn't see all the times
Which then, I thought never would last.

There were gin mills and lots of parties,
I remembered Sadie and Sue,
And Breakwater Bertha even stuck in her pan,
It was cruise number one in review.

Then came a lull in the music,
I felt I'd been hit with a spanner,
Then damn it they started all over again,
This time it was the "Star Spangled Banner".

Oh Hell! I said, "it ain't no use"
They've got me clear down to my shoes,
So I signed again twelve years ago,
That's why I got "Those Shipping Over Blues"

The Weevil

I'm skinny and scrawny, I'm underfed,

47

I used to be husky and big instead,
But they've taken the Weevil out of my bread,
That's what we get in the Navy.

Oh Yes! We've got a modern fleet,
It's new and big and can't be beat,
But they've taken our Weevils and we can't eat,
That's what we get in the Navy.

Why in every bowl of mush we'd get,
We could always find our little pet,
But the bowl is empty where he used to set,
That's what we get in the Navy.

How well I remember, when I used to skim
The top of the milk and wait for him,
Then up he'd pop and start to swim,
That's what we get in the Navy.

There's no more dark spots in our bread,
No bobbing, darting Weevil's head,
In fact they've vanished, all quite dead,
That's what we get in the Navy.

They left our crew in a helluva fix,
When they gave our Weevils the old deep six,
For milk and mush without them don't mix,
That's what we get in the Navy.

It's not that we hate their empty seat,
It's just that we miss our good fresh meat,
And a tasty Weevil can't be beat,
That's what we get in the Navy.

Spell of the Night Wind
The night winds of the desert

Like the night winds of the sea,
Bring thoughts of love and romance,
Drifting serenely by for me.

"Ere I sail on moonlit waters,
Or walk on moonlit sands,
The night winds, stars, and the heaven
Build me love dreams Oh! So grand.

The softest breeze so lightly
Whispers sweet words in my ear,
And in hushed and lusty passion
Caresses cheeks where burns a tear.

Through my hair it ruffles lightly,
Like a maiden's finger tips,
Bringing smiles of sweet contentment
Upon my sore and wearied lips.

Crushes out the fires of hatred,
Soothes my troubled weary soul
With its soft and prayerful sighing,
Like a church hymn it consoles.

"T 'is why I love the night wind,
As it rushes o'er the earth,
For it wraps my soul within itself.
And stills me with its mirth.

South Pacific Heat

God take me back to a climate cool,
For I'm crazed from the heat a ruined fool.
I've cursed it, damned it, felt its gaff.
Then fallen weary and heard its laugh.
Only to rise and fight again,
With heart and soul and tortured limb.

49

In the land of the native's equatorial hell
The heat has whipped me, and cast its spell.
It's spell of dread of the daylight sun
That saps your veins, and cooks you done.
Done in the soul and dead of thought,
Ruined in health from the musty rot.
By the heat of a jungle isle,
Once I stood as you stand there,
Strong and sane without a care,
But that was before the fever came.
And the heat of hell and its companion rain,
They left me then as you see me here,
A bastard breed with a boundless fear,
Warped in body, sick in mind,
All wrought this way by heat, A curse so well defined.

Lonesome Sailor

There is a pale yellow moon hanging high in the sky,
But I'm here in a strange foreign port,
That melancholy mood has me "blue" clear through,
I'm feeling low and all out of sort.

I've been walking the streets since sundown,
My shipmates I left at the dock,
"Cause I'm feeling mighty low and lonesome,
And I have a lump in my throat like a rock.

The people around me are boring, but new;
I guess I should take in the sights,
But that empty old feeling down in my heart
Just draws me away from the lights.

In one bar I wander and out again,
Trying to drown all my feelings in gin,
And always that same old moon above
Keeps drawing me back to those memories within.

My guts take a tumble as I make a pass at a broad,
With her painted up face and wry smile,
So I stumble out to the dark again
To talk with my thoughts for a while.

The hours drag by an endless hell
Been this way since we first hit this hole.
I've not been the same for many a day,
For I am tired with an aching soul.

There is nothing more "blue" than a lonely gob,
He can fight all the elements blast,
But when he feels he's been forgotten back home,
Even this strength can be of the past.

So the silver moon is my buddy,
Alone we stand for worse or better,
And all I ask to be happy once more
Is from home, a long wanted letter.

The Roaming Casanova

Now gather around me lassies and ladies,
Your charms and figures flaunt,
For come the dawn I'm rolling on,
And I must leave no one in want.

My pocketbook is open and ready,
Fortune and fame I give to you,
And a more handsome lad they never had
To sport the Navy Blue.

You can plainly see I'm no braggart,
I'm modest, reserved and genteel,
But I've got a line, the best of its kind,
It's so long it needs a reel.

I've loved 'em, made 'em and left 'em,
All over this battered globe.
I've felt their charms pressed tight in my arms,
Dressed too in some mighty thin robes.

I've left them a twitter and breathless,
Stirred down to their very soul,
I'm a devil I am, but I don't give a damn,
For a heart I've a fiery hot coal.

I've selected, seduced and secured them,
Tied up like a seagoing ship,
They have to give in for they've no chance to win,
And they've some mighty nice dreams for their trip.

So break out the lace and the satin,
Display your seductive charms
To this sailor in blue, who can give to you,
A happy and joyous hour in his arms.

A Soldier's Memories of a Troopship

Body soaked with perspiration.
I lay there in my bunk,
As I dreamed in deathlike stupor,
While the hold around me stunk.

Here in Mid-Pacific,
Like a galley ship of old,
We plowed on to our destiny
In this slimy, stinking hold.

All the hatches had been battened,
And the stale air hung like smoke,
Fit to kill each human being,
For each breath was like a choke.

Here I lay and gazed about me,
My rifle slung below,
And my pack hung by my pillow,
As we wallowed to and fro.

I could hear the men about me,
Smell each body drenched with sweat,
And curse this hell hot troopship,
Which you won't forget, you'll bet.

There were no false ideas of glamour,
As when you sailed to "Auld Lang Syne",
Only heat and heat about you,
And you stunk like barnyard swine.

Oh! The curses that I muttered
As we plowed on o'er the deep,
Then I thought of yet tomorrow,
And I slept a restless sleep.

Freedom's Call

The time has come ye vanquished men,
Rise up and fight to live again,
From this earth go smite the foe
That plagued your land five years ago.
Take pitchfork, gun, or staff in hand,
Drive these sadists from your land.
Wash pure the earth with freedom's blood,
Drive back the killers damning flood.
For who so dies this noted day,
His deeds shall not perish by the way.
Long have you lived 'neath tyrant's rules,
Long been the victim of fascists fools.
Now strike them down and shout again,
We have fought and died as gallant men.

To live and die for justly cause,
Is far better than to live his laws.
Of disbelief and twisted mind,
To save his race he killed your kind,
For ye are men meant to live,
Power of justice the Lord did give.
So men as they could be held in place,
That they might not this earth deface.
Thus, I give you reasons why
To sally forth and across the sky.
Write out this message to all mankind,
Seek out your freedom and ye shall find.

I'm Going Back

When this whole damned mess is over,
When honesty rules supreme,
Then I'm going back to home again,
To do the things I used to dream.

I'm not going to search for wealth,
Or a big and prosperous job,
I'm just going to live a life
That was given to me by God.

'Because I don't believe he wanted
Wars and killing like we do,
For if he did we'd know it,
Of course, that's just my point of view.

But since this fracas started
My soul has ceased to live,
I've gone and killed like others,
And hope he will forgive.

Yes, I've missed the things I used to do,
Of course, they weren't so much,

Just going hunting and fishing,
A county fair or two, and such.

But it is not the things I did,
It's the kick I got from them,
And like I said before,
I'm aiming to do them all again

PART II -MEMORIES

Reflections of a Grand Reunion

I wrote the following to two of my cousins, who initiated the action that brought about the reunion. This is my personal remembrance of the occasion.

On two vivid days, the Third and Fourth of July, 1990, the past came alive at "Granny Jones" old home in Hailey, Idaho. It was as if 50 years had melted away, and we were kids again.

As I parked the motor home, I caught a glimpse of the old home in its entire splendor. The big old cottonwood tree was gone, as was the maple, it's frozen, sweet icicles I used to suck on in the winter. However, there behind the lilac trees with its white walls and pretty blue porch, the old house beckoned.

The two cousins and their father greeted me. I had seen them last in 1940, when I was home on "boot" leave from the Navy. The girls had grown into lovely charming ladies, and their father had aged gracefully. What a warm feeling this left in me.

We talked and talked. As the days passed, others began to arrive. Cousins and their children from Washington, Colorado, Utah, Idaho and Alaska appeared. The great dedication to this reunion was obvious. There were the Bolligers, Hackers, Mills, Werrys, Hermans, Moores, Vaneks, Loves, Jones and Kippers and the Hamelraths to name a few. Also present were the close friends of the family, who in their love chose to come. Aunt Alma Reeder, of course, was the "Guest of Honor", still witty and sharp with her humor.

The flow of memory stories about the old house and especially loveable "Granny" Jones flowed like vintage wine. We were intoxicated with the headiness of the past. I could not but feel sad that the young ones playing in the yard, and even their young parents never knew the joy of "Granny" Jones. Her caring, loving ways with never a sharp word said about anyone, her cooking that never ceased to please, an experience of a life they never would be able to enjoy.

On the Fourth of July, we all attended the parade. The "Fourth" in Hailey was always a focal point for the families. I recounted that sixty years ago on this day I first came to Hailey. I met many of these cousins for the first time on that day.

Lois and Joannie, the hosts, had restored the old home to much of its old style. The back yard, with its memories of long ago, was where we all gathered for the picnic. The food was delicious, and the selection seemed endless. I could not help but recall a winter in the 1930's depression when we lived in this old house and there was no food on hand. Today we had more cheerful things to talk about, as we filled our plates with the goodies.

The conversations glided by endlessly. We talked of marriages and deaths, careers, births and just happenings. Voices grew hoarse from unaccustomed, lengthy conversation.

Inevitably the time arrived when all of this lovely happening had to end. One by one the family of Jones began to go the separate ways of diverse families. Hugs and kisses followed with pledges made to visit or write more often. The crowd thinned one by one, and the silence set in. The emptiness of the quiet dissolved the past in one fell swoop, and it was again July 4, 1990.

I stood and looked at the circle of empty chairs that sat in the backyard. My thoughts were, "There sit the ghosts of Fourth of July's Past". So many of us on this day had enjoyed the old house and "Granny Jones". It was the highlight of the summer; now it was over and we could only thank Lois and Joannie from the bottom of our hearts for making it all happen

The Day Hawaii Lost Its Innocence

It was 7 December, 1941, the hour 0700; and a beautiful Sunday morning. I had recently awakened, dressed and prepared for my day of duty. I proceeded to the seaplane deck and aft to the seaplane crane for an early morning look at the island of Oahu. My ship, USS Tangier (AV- 8), was moored at berth F10 at Ford Island, which contained the Navy airfield; the island was in the center of Pearl Harbor.

I was alone on the seaplane deck; there was almost total silence. The only sound that floated on the slight breeze across the quiet bay was a slow chug chugging of a motor launches engine as the launch proceeded to some dock within the inner harbor.

I stood there mesmerized by the quiet beauty of Hawaii. The sugar cane and pineapple fields rose gently in green profusion to the cloud topped mountains that formed the backbone of the island. I could see the outline of the path through the cane fields where the narrow gauge railway ran.

This was the Hawaii that I had dreamed of, when I saw the Navy Enlistment Posters in my hometown of Twin Falls, Idaho. It was all there, even in my mind I saw the hula skirt clad girls of the islands, and heard the melodious strum of the Hawaiian guitars. In eleven days I would be twenty years old, what a gift for a birthday present. With these thoughts and the beauty of the morning fresh in my mind I proceeded to the mess deck for breakfast.

I remember only one item of the breakfast menu, Kadota Figs, which I still love and can seldom find. There was the usual small talk with shipmates; one seldom had time for long conversations as the mess deck master-at -arms kept the crew moving so all could be fed in the allotted time for meals. I had completed my meal and was emptying my mess tray, when the General Alarm sounded for battle stations. The beauty of that morning, still fresh in my mind, was suddenly ripped from me by the call to "General Quarters", never to return again.

Within a matter of minutes our guns began to fire; I had dashed down the ladder to the main engine room to assist in lighting off the main engines in preparation to get underway if ordered. In a matter of minutes the word was passed that we were under attack by aircraft of the Japanese Empire. In this short period of time we had gone from peace and tranquility to total war.

The attack lasted about an hour and a half. During the attack the Captain kept the engine room personnel apprised of the action up on deck. Four bombs had been dropped at the ship, but narrowly missed. The vibrations from the explosions were terrific, and we were not sure if we had been hit or not, until the Captain told us they were near misses. One torpedo had been launched at us but it also missed. The ship had downed three planes and assisted with the sinking of a two-man submarine off our starboard bow. Our gunners had put a three inch round through the sub's conning tower; the final blow had been completed by the USS Monaghan DD354 with a depth charge attack.

At last the attacking planes cleared the area. At approximately 1100 a few of us below deck were allowed to go topside and view the damage sustained to the ships and installations. The carnage was unbelievable. Smoke and fire were everywhere; the old battleship Utah astern of us was capsized. The cruiser Raleigh ahead of Utah was stern down from a bomb or torpedo hit. Across Ford Island the Arizona was burning, damage sustained by other ships was obscured by the smoke of the burning oil on the water. Tangier had suffered only strafing damage from the attacking planes. The near misses from the bombs had caused only superficial damage to the hull.

The commanding officer of our ship, Cdr. C.A.F. Sprague, dispatched our ship's launches to help retrieve the wounded and floating dead of the sunken ships. Our Shipfitters were busy trying to free men from the inside of the capsized Utah. In spite of the total chaos work was progressing in an orderly manner.

As I stood there on the seaplane deck surveying this hell's inferno my eyes shifted to the sugar cane and pineapple fields, now barely visible because of the fire and smoke. The beautiful scene I had observed only four hours before was now gone. I suddenly realized that I had the privilege, for a few brief moments, of seeing Hawaii in its final innocent beauty. The Hawaii of the sugar cane and pineapple barons would be no more, as would the tiny narrow gauge railway. That last glimpse that I had of Hawaii just a short time ago was gone. War had suddenly come and changed in a few hours what for centuries God had given us. That was the day boys became men, men became heroes, and Hawaii lost its innocence.

Palm Grove "Ballroom"

It was late January or early February, 1945, my ship USS Tangier AV 8, was anchored off Cabalitian Island, Lingayen Gulf, Luzon, Philippine, Islands supporting our attached squadron of PBY and PBM patrol bombers. The war was slowly moving closer to the Japanese Mainland, and our troops were moving steadily up the Island of Luzon. At night you could hear the rumble of artillery fire and see the flashes of explosions on the island.

Planes from our aircraft carriers and our land based aircraft had cleared the skies of Japanese planes in our area. It was a welcome break from our recent deployment. A short time before, we had been engaged with the enemy at Moratai Island. This area was near the Japanese held Halmahera Islands. In our new anchorage recreation groups of sailors from my ship were allowed time ashore for a couple of beers and relaxation. I had no idea that in the few days that followed a more surprising bit of entertainment would be offered to members of the crew who wanted to participate.

When the Japanese invaded the Philippines at the beginning of the war in 1941, many of the Filipinos had fled the cities to the out-lying islands, taking with them what cherished possessions they could carry. A group of musicians had fled to the area near our present anchorage, bringing their instruments with them. This group of musicians had volunteered to play for us when we came ashore for our two beers. Their first stop was the Officers area, then the Chief Petty Officers and finally for us, the white hats. It was great to hear good music, and they knew all the old songs that were popular before the war.

One morning it was announced that any member of the crew who wanted to attend a dance ashore would be granted permission to attend. There were few who had any interest, but I thought this would be great and volunteered. I never thought where the dance could or would be held. A few of us decided it would be nice to take some gift or offering of appreciation with us, so we talked the baker out of some fresh baked bread. We also brought a couple of bottles of coca cola from the gedunk stand (soda fountain). We were sure these gifts would be welcomed after all the hardships the Filipino people must have suffered over the past four years of occupation and war. At 1300 on the day of the dance the word was passed that the boat for the beach was ready to depart. It was a short ride to the beach, and as I recall we did not converse very much on what to expect once we arrived at the dance area, where ever that might be. We were greeted by a Filipino man on our arrival and instructed to follow him. He led us a short distance into the palm tree grove where the ground had been packed as hard as concrete. It was obvious this was to be the dance area. We stood there briefly looking around, when slowly the Filipino girls began to arrive. One by one they appeared from out of the palm grove, each one accompanied by her chaperone. It was obvious there would be no hanky panky with the sailors.

The appearance of the girls was one of the most impressive sights I had ever witnessed. They were dressed in elegant formal dresses like queens of a formal ball. The site took all of us by surprise. How did these young ladies acquire such lovely gowns? It was explained, that when they fled from their homes at the start of the Japanese invasion of their country they simply took them along as they departed. It was such an incredible thing to see, and I have never forgotten it. I felt so humbled by this grand gesture, and the memories have stayed with me for sixty-nine years. The appearance of these young ladies and their chaperones certainly subdued any raucous nature we young sailors might have entertained. I remembered that the Philippine Islands had at one time been under Spanish rule, and the regal demeanor of these young ladies and their grand gowns were all part of this heritage.

The dance was a great success, and the music provided by the band took all of us back before the war, when as kids we attended our high school proms. The packed earth created no problems with our dancing. The conversation was congenial as the girls spoke fluent English. The afternoon wore by so quickly; it was like something out of a fairy story book. For just a few brief hours the war was someplace else and we were at the "Ball".

Sixty-Seven Years Together With a Wonderful Wife

It seems incredible that two young people could be cast together on a cold, rainy February night, and eventually walk the path of life, as one, for sixty-seven years. I cannot ever express what these years have meant to me. You were the love I needed to fill the emptiness in my being. From the moment we met, I knew I would love you. You have given me comfort, love, friendship, support in all my endeavors, and confidence in my capabilities when I was sometimes in doubt. You gave us a wonderful daughter and raised her into a lovely and competent young lady. When I was away at sea, you were the anchor that held our household together; I always knew things were in good hands. You never wanted beyond our meager means, you always accepted what we had, and many times, it was not much, but we continued to love each other through the lean times. I want you to know that I love you and always will to a depth I will never be able to find words to express. I can only say, "thank you precious one for all of this love you have given me". If I am cross or short tempered at times, it is my weakness and I always regret my quick words, but please accept my apology for the times this has happened. I know that my simple stupidity has hurt you and always suffer inwardly when it happens. You are and will always be my precious one, my sweetheart. Thank you darling for all of these wonderful years together

The Day "God" Gave me Another Chance

The morning of Monday, 8 February, 1960, for me, began no differently than any other. The Marine Troops in the compartment the next deck above me awakened me when their boots hit the deck. The noise was always enough to get one out of his bunk. I had grudgingly become accustomed to this clatter; I could have had a room lower in the ship, but I would have had to share it with another officer, and I liked my privacy in spite of the noise.

I was embarked in USS Boxer LPH-4, which was the Flag Ship of Amphibious Squadron Ten. I was assigned as the Staff Material Officer. The Boxer was a World War II Essex Class Aircraft Carrier; she had served as a CV, CVS and now as an LPH. An LPH was a

Helicopter carrier designated to land Marine Troops ashore as part of an amphibious landing. The Navy and the Marine Corps were vigorously pursuing the perfection of vertical deployment of troops as part of Amphibious Warfare. The Marine Brigade that was currently aboard had deployed out of Camp Lejeune, North Carolina; this was my first deployment since reporting for duty the previous September. Fidel Castro had just taken control of Cuba the previous year, and this probably was why the squadron was deployed in the area.

The USS Boxer was anchored off the Island of Vieques, which lies due east of Puerto Rico. On this particular day, the Marine Brigade was going to conduct a live fire demonstration on the island. This island had been used by the Navy for years for shore bombardment practice. The Amphibious Squadron Chief Staff Officer, Cdr. Sam Jones, had decided that members of the staff should go ashore and observe the demonstration as an element of staff orientation and training. We would debark by helicopter, as this was the element of transport used by the troops and our reason for existence as a unit. I was looking forward to the flight; I had flown in a helicopter only once before, and it was a small three passenger one. The Bell Aircraft Company had offered demonstration rides to members of the staff shortly after I joined the command, and I was given the chance to be one of the recipients.

The departure time, as I remember, was about mid-day. The flight consisted of three helicopters in order to accommodate all the members of the staff and one or two officers from the Boxer. The lift-off was uneventful and the flight to the island landing zone was a relatively short one. The LZ was atop a mountain ridge, and it was from this site that we were to observe the firing demonstration. In spite of the altitude of the LZ, it was hot and I was not really interested in the firing. I had seen such demonstrations before I entered the Navy; I had been in the Idaho National Guard and witnessed Artillery fire, which was not all that different from what I was currently observing. The afternoon wore on, eventually the demonstration ended and it was time to return to the Boxer. It was getting close to mealtime on the ship, so the helicopters flew us back to the island's Marine Camp for evening chow. The food was served field style, but good. Prior to our meal, we were afforded the opportunity for a couple of drinks and time to talk with our Marine counterparts.

The evening wore on and finally it was time to embark our assigned helicopter and return to the ship. I was ready, for it had been a long day, with a lot of just standing and waiting, and I was looking forward to getting into my bunk. I climbed aboard my assigned bird, put on my Mae West Lifejacket and took my seat on the port side and just forward of the cargo door, which was on the starboard side of the helicopter. Sitting next to me was the Gunnery Officer of the USS Boxer, LCDR Miller. Between LCDR Miller and me was a stowed life raft, and being tired I put my head down on it and started to doze.

The lift-off was routine and we soared off into the pitch- blackness of the night for our short flight back to the ship. The constant roar of the helicopter engine, in spite of its noise, lulled me into a light sleep. I could hear the whop, whop, whop of the rotor blades directly over my seat and thought to myself we will be on the flight deck soon. The next thing I heard was someone of our staff, who was also onboard but further aft, shouting to jump that we were going down. This was repeated several times calling out my nickname, "Ham" to jump.

I stood up, and as I did, I could hear the louder roar of the helicopter engines as the pilot, Captain, USMC tried to add more collective to the rotor blades in an effort to gain altitude. I instinctively activated the CO_2 cartridges in my Mae West, and at the same time the thought going through my mind was don't jump you will get caught in the rotor blades. The other members of the staff had already jumped. My hesitation in jumping and inflating my life jacket was conducted in a matter of seconds. In the next instant, we had hit the water; there was no flotation time for the helicopter. It flooded immediately and began a swift decent to the bottom of the bay.

The rush of seawater through the open hatch was like a tidal wave. I had lunged for the door, but immediately became buoyant because of my inflated Mae West. The helicopter in essence was sinking with me. I had become hung up at the top of the door; the helicopter was on top of my neck and I could not get free. In spite of the total darkness, I could still see the line between the rushing water and the night sky. The escaping air bubbles from inside the craft were clearly visible; I could see the skyline quickly disappearing and I cried out loud in fear and desperation" Jesus Christ Not Like This". Was it a blasphemy or a prayer? That was the last I remember as I blacked out into unconsciousness. (I later realized that drowning could be a relatively painless way to die).

In times of emergencies, or so it seems, that a set of circumstances can exist that set about a plan of recovery that if planned could not exceed what fate dictated. Such was the case on Boxer when the accident occurred. The time was a few minutes before 2200, the time of the day when the ship's Chaplain came to the quarterdeck to give the evening prayer over the ship's loudspeaker system. The Boxer was destined to sortie the next morning for exercises with other ships of the squadron. She had hoisted in all of her boats except one motor launch, because of the timing of the Chaplain's prayer the Officer of the Deck had ordered the coxswain of the motor launch to lay off until after the prayer. At that time, the launch would be hoisted aboard. Added to this the crew of the signal bridge was alert and monitoring the approach of the helicopters. As soon as it was evident that the helicopter had crashed the signal crew immediately directed a beam from a searchlight on the crash area. At the same time the Officer of the Deck ordered the launch that was still in the water to proceed to the scene to recover the survivors. By this set of coincidences a quick recovery of the victims was accomplished. (I learned of these particulars after I had recovered from my injuries and had returned to the staff for duty).

The men who had jumped from the aircraft were quickly found and brought into the launch. They told me later they had to look around a bit before I was found. My Mae West Life Jacket was properly inflated, but contrary to normal procedures I was floating face down in the water, but they told me later my uniform cap was still on my head. I was properly dressed even during dire circumstances. I was unconscious.

My first moment when I became lucid enough to recognize my surroundings was when they were carrying me up the gangway in a Stokes stretcher. I vaguely remember the face of the Officer of The Deck, Captain Fichter, (sp) USMC, and then I became unconscious again. Once in Sickbay there were moments when I was in and out of it again, but I do remember someone saying he has to be transported to the hospital in San Juan, in Puerto Rico. Once more on the flight deck I became conscious and knew they were putting me in another helicopter for the flight to the hospital, and I uttered another expletive about having to go in one of them again. The next day I regained consciousness in the hospital; I was in an oxygen tent and remained there for three days.

The extent of my injuries consisted of bleeding from both ears, ruptured eardrums and chemical pneumonia, which was caused by my ingesting aviation gasoline and seawater. The ruptured eardrums was caused by the rapid compression and decompression from the pressure generated by the depth to which I had submerged, before I came clear of the wreckage. This depth was estimated to be a minimum of fifty feet. The neck vertebra that was injured, by my having been forced against the top of the hatch, was caused by inflating my Mae West too soon. This did not bother me until 1968. The chemical pneumonia was cured in a matter of days. My hearing was modified for weeks after the accident. The affect of shock lasted for a long time, and I was amazed how debilitating it can be. Physically I was weak for quite some time; I became tired very easily.

I spent two weeks in the US Army Rodriguez Hospital in San Juan. On the day of my discharge I had orders to return to the Staff on the Boxer, which was back in Norfolk, Virginia. While I was waiting at the control tower at the airfield I was informed my flight had been cancelled. I returned to my room at the Bachelor Officer's Quarters and waited for further instructions, they were soon to arrive. I was issued a commercial ticket on a Pan American Airways flight. There was hurried ride to the airport. The door of the plane was closing when the Navy station wagon arrived at the loading platform.

I was acutely aware of my personal appearance, which embarrassed me, as I hurriedly boarded the plane. I was dressed in dress khakis with blouse and necktie, even under normal circumstances it was uncomfortably hot in Puerto Rico's tropic weather. In my weakened condition and having to carry my suitcase I was sweating profusely. I certainly did not present a very good military appearance. My embarrassment was further amplified by the fact that the plane was fully loaded and every face seemed to be turned in my direction. I was happy to sink into my seat hoping to fade from the view of all of the eyes staring at me.

I was not keen on flying back, somehow I had lost my zest for flying. This was soon to be exacerbated when the Flight Stewardess dropped the morning paper in my lap shortly after takeoff; there in bold headlines were the words, "Navy Plane Crashes at Rio de Janerio, 11 members of Navy Band Killed". That was the plane I was supposed to fly on to the states. I flew many times after the accident, but was never comfortable; I flew mainly because duty required me to do so.

There were two casualties as a result of the crash. Corporal Henry Taylor Jr., USMC died from head injuries. I have often wondered if he had jumped from the helicopter and was hit by the rotor blades. LCDR. Miller, USN, who sat next to me in the helicopter, suffered a heart attack. They recovered his body the next day on the bottom of the bay at the crash site. The helicopter, HRS 81, was salvaged by a U S Navy Salvage vessel. I have a picture of it taken right after it was recovered, it hangs on the wall in our den.

I did not know until I returned home, after my recovery, that the pilot of the helicopter and the Crew Chief, were also admitted for injuries they received. The extent of their injuries I never knew. I did find out that the Crew Chief made a miraculous escape by going from his station in the cargo/troop space up through the cockpit area and out the canopy opening. A feat I am sure he was able to perform as a result of his training. The pilot, later in life, became a test pilot, whether military or civilian I never learned.

There are two things that I continue to ponder. Did the Good Lord accept my uttered expletive at the time of the crash as a curse or as a prayer for survival, and the other did LCDR Miller sacrifice his life to push me free of the helicopter hatch.

The question posed was, why did I inflate my Mae West before I was clear of the aircraft. Strange as it may seem I never ever received instructions as to when I should inflate it. All during World War II, I carried a CO_2 inflatable life belt, and wore it below decks during every battle situation at General Quarters. I can only imagine what the consequences would have been if the ship was sinking, and I made the same misjudgment I made in the helicopter.

There was very poor communication and follow-up with the families of the injured and deceased. My wife, Rose Ann, received four brief telegrams vaguely outlining my injuries. There were no personal calls by any member of the Naval Service and no reports as to my progress of recovery. The Chaplain assigned to the Staff of Commander Amphibious Force Atlantic, which was located in Little Creek, Virginia, did not make any courtesy calls, even to the wife of deceased LCDR George Miler. Amphibious Squadron Ten was assigned to Commander Amphibious Force Atlantic. I remembered this at my next duty assignment after leaving Amphibious Squadron Ten. I was ordered to duty as Commanding Officer of the US Naval and Marine Corps Reserve Training Center in Butte, Montana. One of my collateral duties was Casualty Assistance Calls Officer. This duty consisted of handling all injuries or deaths of Navy Personnel in my area of responsibility, which was the greater portion of Western Montana. I never forgot the importance of personal contact and always made sure the families of the injured or deceased received the attention they so richly deserved. One of the most gratifying moments of my life was when the families expressed their appreciation of this attention to duty. I have been blessed twice, to say the least.

The Road

Soft snow sifted down under my collar as I tried to pull myself deeper into the warmth of my old Navy N-4 jacket. I hunched myself under the raised hood of my pickup, trying to coax the cold quart of oil into the engine. The late spring storm, which had blown into the valley during the night, was beginning to wear itself out. I was anxious to get inside to the warmth of the restaurant and breakfast. It was getting time to get on the road.

As I looked out over the engine, I saw the road. It was US Highway 93, which headed North from Wells, Nevada, where we had spent the night; the road we were going to take. Highway 93 crossed Interstate 80 at this point. It was at this moment that the cold, the snow, and the lonely road came together in one blending of memories. Once again, in my mind, it was February, 1944, and I was headed home on a short leave from the war in the Pacific. It was my first return to the states in over a year.

Wells, Nevada was the point where I changed from the Greyhound Bus from Oakland, California to the Sun Valley, Idaho/ Wells, Nevada Stage. This would take me to my home in Twin Falls, Idaho. The Oakland Bus would continue on to Salt Lake City, Utah.

I had not been home on leave from the war since August of 1942; the road would take me there.

My wife, Rose, and I hurriedly finished our breakfast, eager to get on our way while there was a break in the weather, we still had a long way to go. We would only be passing through my old home town of Twin Falls, Idaho. We had driven this route before, but this was the first time nostalgia had raised its head, the road beckoned like a grasping hand.

Departure from Wells was up a slight incline in the road as it headed North to higher elevation. In the beginning the road seemed as it used to be, but the further we went the more changes I noticed. We passed an old horse ranch that I remembered, the buildings by the

71

highway were now dilapidated and weather worn, and the road now was beginning to take its old route. I felt isolated when I watched it slip away over a slight rise out into the desert of sagebrush. The new road was wider and straighter, but the old memories were with that old departed section of road. We continued and not far up the highway I caught a glimpse of my old friend meandering back to us.

This on and off departure and return continued for miles, here with us for a while and then silently leaving for a route much easier to build back when it was first constructed. Frequently the road would disappear, vanish completely from sight, but then reappear as a faint discernible line on a distant hillside and then sweep over a ridge and return running parallel to our course. The old asphalt was beginning to crumble and bits of sagebrush and weeds, of all sorts, were beginning to take over its surface. We passed the old Mineral Wells Hot Springs Resort, now closed and dying, but there was the old road passing close by the old relic of buildings, going on its separate way pulling my memories of a day long past with it. In my mind's eye I could still see the old Sun Valley Stage chugging away around the bends and up and down the hills ever drawing me closer to home.

I kept pointing out to Rose, places that I remembered; I am sure I bored her with my reminiscence. At one point the old stone building that was a stage stop and a bar emerged from the sagebrush, and I remembered having a Tom Collins and a short dance to the juke box music. The stonewalls were still standing, and continued to support what was left of a sagging roof. If one listened one could hear the silent notes coming from within from the juke box music of the war years.

Eventually we left the hilly desert behind and descended to the little town of Rogerson, Idaho, still just a wide spot in the road, but we were back on the route of the old road. As we drove along getting closer to my hometown, I remembered off to the right where the National Guard firing range was located, and where as a member of the rifle team I spent happy hours improving my skills. Yes, the old road and I were one again.

Twin Falls finally came into view and we had left my old friend, the road behind. We drove through town and on to Taylor Street, and there on the narrow tree lined street was number 175. It was a small house, but neatly built and the present owners had treated it well. This was the only house my parents ever had, and they had bought it in 1939. I lived there until June of 1940 when I left home for the Navy. There were many sad times spent there, but in spite of all the heartaches it was still my home. I thank you old road for bringing me back for even a fleeting moment of passing.

My wife and I have driven the road between Wells and Twin Falls many times over the years and I still can trace the old road as it weaves its way back and forth across the new road. The old friend is fading with time, but the memories of coming home over it have remained.

Memories of A Young Marine

Responsibility sometimes develops odd mental habits, and over my thirty years of service in the navy, I experienced such a development. It began very simply of going over all the daily requirements of my position as an enlisted ship's engineer, and later as a commissioned office. In my mind, I would analyze the action I had taken to correct some engineering problem of the day, or to contemplate what needed to be done to solve a still existing one. This mental process would begin as soon as I went to bed. It continues to this day, but now memories, unrelated to engineering, slowly evolve from the voluminous folds of the human brain. These thoughts cover events so distant that I am amazed at their recall. It is a habit at times that can drain me of a good night's rest, however, it continues to this day. The following event has come to mind many times, and though only a fleeting happening it has left an indelible imprint in the mind of my past.

The battle for the Japanese Island of Guadalcanal had been in progress since August of 1942. It was the first major amphibious invasion by the United States Forces in the tenaciously held territories of the Japanese Forces in the South Pacific. It had been a fierce continuous effort and the US had lost many ships in its efforts to capture, and defend the island with its much needed airfield. Once in US hands it would provide an airfield for land based fighter and bomber support for our troops.

My ship, USS Tangier AV-8, a large PBY Patrol Bomber Tender, was anchored at her advanced base of operations in the Group of Islands known as the New Hebrides, which are approximately 800 miles south-south east of Guadalcanal. It was now late 1942 or early 1943 when a Detachment of Marines arrived on board en route to an area for refitting and rest.

They were a battle worn looking group, tired, dirty and uniforms that revealed long days of no changing and deterioration from the battles and the unrelenting jungle rot. It was obvious they had spent some time in hell, still looking defiant but quietly subdued in their conversation. Once aboard they were met by members of our crew, who assisted them as best they could.

It was at this time that I observed a young Marine standing alone, seemingly not able to comprehend where he was. I slowly approached him, introduced myself, and asked him if he would like a shower. He looked at me and nodded. I then asked him from where he had come, and what type of organization to which he was attached. He replied he was part of an Anti-Aircraft Defense Gun Crew. He talked quietly, and I had the common sense not to press for details. I am not sure we even exchanged names.

Once he showered, I gave him a pair of my navy dungarees and shirt and scivvies (underwear), at this time I was a Machinist Mate Second Class. I treated him to some ice cream at the geedunk stand (soda fountain). The blank look on his face had not diminished. His eyes were trying to tell me a story, but I would not bring myself to the point of asking stupid questions. I asked him how old he was, he replied seventeen, and I knew this young Marine had seen and witnessed some vestiges of a hell he would never forget. I was twenty-one, and in his presence I suddenly felt like he needed an older brother, but I could not, and would not try to cross that line. He was so gaunt, weighing I would estimate 110 pounds at the most, but the eyes and the face transfixed my attention; I could not shake my focus.

We stood together and talked idly for a short while; he never seemed to accept where he was, and at this moment all the noise of hell, he had shared with his fellow Marines was now behind him, at least for what time would allow. His closeness and demeanor seemed to try to pull me into his inner self and wanting to absorb his feelings. I had never suffered such a feeling of helplessness towards another human being. So young was he and so impressively remote from his reality.

Our quiet meeting was interrupted when a Sergeant of his Marine group suddenly made his presence known by shouting orders for all Marines to fall in and prepare to leave the ship. The young Marine smiled, thanked me and in his still battle-warped daze fell in with the group as they headed for the ship's gangway to debark. The last words I heard were the Marine Sergeant vehemently berating my short time friend; his words were, "what the hell are you doing in navy uniform, damn it you are a Marine, get out of those clothes".

To this day, those words still echo in my mind, and I think once a Marine always a Marine. That is their purpose of training; in "boot" camp, they strip you of all your identity and then bring you back as they want you, a full- fledged mental convert to the "Corps". That is what makes them unique, however, that brief friend of mine, and his battle -punished mind, is and will forever be in my velvet clouded memory as long as I live. I will always wonder if he made it all the way, or did his punished youth fail him on some other South Pacific beachhead.

A Tribute to our Daughter Linda

Dearest Linda,

Six decades ago two young people in love and inexperienced in the art of parenting were presented with a bundle of joy that would forever

75

change and enhance the very meaning of their lives; that bundle of joy was you. We fretted over you with your colic and inability to hold down your food. Mom with her ever present persevering found a formula that you could tolerate and then you began to grow, and as you grew so did we as parents. You were an ever smiling, bubbling bundle of love, a joy to hold and admire. You were our lovely baby daughter.

Time seemed to pass too quickly, you grew from that chubby little baby into a toddler who loved to hijack tricycles from the neighbor kids. When we took you to Sears and Roebuck to buy you your own, you threw a tantrum when we took you off the one we had you ride to see if it was your size. You thought you were not going to get it. We managed to get you and the tricycle into the car and home and life returned to normal.

In no time, you were in school and always a fine student, you loved school and mom and I were proud of you. You always managed to maintain good grades whenever a move was required. This continued through all your grade school years and high school. Mom and I were always so proud of you.

One of the finest qualities you were born with, and continued to develop as you grew into a mature young lady, was your sense of humor and love of other people. Never in all the years did you ever cause any concern or problems for your mom or dad. You were and are a wonderful daughter. Your artistic ability is ever present, when one enters your home to see the subject of your creative décor. Once again, we are proud of what you accomplish.

You have given us so many fond memories and to your family you have given an environment of love, compassion, understanding and guidance that is rarely found in our society today. We have never stopped thinking of you as our "babes" and never will.

We deeply regret we cannot be with you on this memorable day, not just because it is your birthday, but rather a day on which you are to be honored for all the achievements you have made as our daughter, as a faithful and caring wife, a wonderful mother, and above all else a beloved human being.

Happy Birthday Dearest Linda, may you continue to have many more years of a rich and rewarding life, which you so rightly deserve. Remember, "Life is a Journey" not a Destination. Lovingly, Mom and Dad

Predestined Rendezvous

The rain pelting down on the metal cover of the boat engine, along with the noise it made contacting the metal hull of the boat sounded like shotgun pellets. It was a foul February night in 1946, and not a good night to be out and about. I stood in the boat with my back toward the bow looking aft at the black outline of my ship moored to a dock at Todd Shipyard in Seattle, Washington. We had just returned from a trip to Yokohama, Japan to bring home troops from the war, which had ended just a few months earlier. We were in the shipyard for an upkeep period for minor repairs.

The boat I was in was headed for the dock near the Ferry Landing at Seattle's water front. The boat, as well as the ship I had just left, was not real navy. The ship was a large passenger/cargo ship designed in 1939 for Maritime service; it was a P3 hull design, as I recall, and could carry 5,000 troops at a speed of 22 knots. There were ten of them built as the Admiral Class Transports; the ship I was assigned to was the Admiral Hugh Rodman AP126, which had been commissioned in mid-1945. These ships were built and commissioned to carry large amounts of troops, if we were to invade Japan, which luckily never had to happen. The boat I was in was also of Maritime vintage, with a four -cylinder gas engine and a metal hull and the only thing Navy about it was the grey paint. This was not the type of ship I had wanted when I was transferred from the USS Tangier AV8 in February of 1945. At the time, the ship was at Mindoro Island in the Philippines. I had longed for a ship of the line of new construction, but I guess the Navy was taking care of me. I had survived the attack at Pearl Harbor, so they relegated me to safer waters.

The drenching rain had penetrated the topcoat I was wearing, and turning my back to the torrent gave no relief. I was slowly getting soaked to my inner uniform. The Navy never had regulation raincoats until several years later; the topcoats were great for looks but not very utilitarian. I had left the ship to get away from the silent loneliness of the ship. The ship was just a vast empty shell when all the troops were gone. The crew of the ship barely made a dent in the vastness of that empty hull. I was headed for the Trianon Ballroom in Seattle, a nice place to dance I was told. The Trianon was located on 3rd Avenue and Wall Streets, which was a good walk from the Ferry Landing, and I had to walk as I only had a pittance in my pocket for expenses.

The streets of the city were quiet as I made my way up the hill to 3rd Avenue where I turned North towards Wall Street. People with any good sense would not be out on such a rainy night. Eventually my journey through the city on this wet night brought me to the entrance to the ballroom, and by this time, I was really wet. I reached for the handle of the door and noticed the sign, which stated it was Monday night, Big Name Band night, and the admission was two dollars instead of the usual one dollar. I only had five dollars in my pocket and payday was still down the road, for a few brief seconds I mulled this over in my mind and then figured it was worth the extra dollar just to go in and dry out.

Once inside I took off my topcoat and checked it with the check girl, then made my way to the edge of the dance floor. Gene Krupa's band was playing that night and there was a large crowd in attendance. Krupa's music was always loud and fast, and he on his drums was always the showcase person. He played his talent and ego to the hilt. I managed to ask a girl for my first dance of the evening, which was a fast number and difficult to dance, with Krupa's noise and showmanship. The dance completed I returned to the stag line.

I stood at the edge of the dance floor and gazed at the unaccompanied girls standing on the other side and tried to decide whom I would ask for the next dance The music had just started when I saw a girl who caught my eye, and I immediately hurried over to ask her for the dance. She agreed to dance and we whirled away to the sound of the music of "Oh What It Seemed to Be", which became popular by Frankie Carl. As we danced we chatted and exchanged small talk, and there was something about this girl that was different, refined, quiet in her own way and very pretty. Her name was Rose Ann Lucas, and she was from Wardner, Idaho, which was a mining town in northern Idaho. I liked her from our first encounter, and as the evening passed, we shared each dance. We talked of our hometowns, the things we liked to do and our love of the out-of-doors. There was no doubt we had a lot in common; by evenings end I knew I had to see this girl again.

We told each other how we had managed to be at the ballroom; she had promised to go with some of her friends sometime before this particular evening, and then at the last minute she said she was not going, but her friends said you promised so she changed her mind and decided to go. I told her I had walked all the way from the Ferry Building in the rain and when I got there, I saw the admission was twice the normal amount and almost did not come in. I told her because I was so wet from the rain I figured it was worth the amount just to dry off. We both laughed at that.

The dance music finally ended, and I asked her if I could escort her home, she lived with some of her friends at the Haddon Hall Apartment Hotel. We waited in front of the ballroom for the city bus to arrive and then I rode with her to her hotel. We talked a bit, I kissed her good night and asked for a date the next evening, but she said she already had made a date with someone. I was shattered and filled with childish jealousy, which I had no right to feel. The next evening I sat in a restaurant across the street from her hotel waiting to see whom she had dated. They never showed up or I was a day late and a dollar short. I was afraid I would never see her again. I had fallen for this girl and I knew she was going to be the one for me.

She had shown all of the qualities that I had ever hoped for in a girl, a lady. She was that in every way. She did agree to a date with me a few days later, and thus began our courting.

In March of that year, I reenlisted in the Navy, a few days later I bought the engagement and wedding ring and asked her to marry me. She said yes and the rest is history. To date we have been married sixty-seven years, and I will always remember that predestined rendezvous.

The Journey
Maine to Spain by the Way of Arkansas

This is a quote I learned from an old shipmate; it sort if explains why this trip became a journey.

The hands on the clock on the wall of the machine shop stood at 1500 navy time (3:00 PM). My work for the day had been completed. I was anxiously awaiting the start of liberty at 1600 hours. My thirty days leave was to start at 0800 the next morning, but I had wrangled a deal, where they would let me leave on this day and log me out the next morning. That would give me a few hours extra to get a head start, for I had a long ways to go. Kellogg, Idaho was a long ways from Key West, Florida, where I was stationed. It was December, 1947 and I wondered what winter road conditions lay ahead.

As I stood killing time, until liberty started, I began to think back on the many months I prepared this trip for my wife, Rose, our six weeks old daughter, Linda, and me and the car. The real task had been preparing the thirteen year old Chevrolet. I had never overhauled a car, knew little or nothing about all that was required, and had only owned one car before this one, and that for only a brief time. I did have my navy machinist's mate school experience on which to rely. I tackled the job, with the help of an eleven hundred page Dykes Automobile Encyclopedia, which contained information on car repair dating back to the first cars built, and a friend, who was a Chief Engineman.

I worked for eight months rebuilding the entire engine, and rewiring the car one wire at a time. I decided this needed to be done when one night the headlights went out and replacing the fuse did not correct the problem. I figured it had to be the wires, so I talked a Chief Electronic Technician, a shipmate of mine, to lend me some wire, (a loose phrase to say the least). The wire was of one color code so the only way I could rewire the car was to take one wire out and put one wire back. I still think what a job it would have been for someone, other than me, to trouble shoot such a wiring set-up. In the end, this did not correct the initial problem, which turned out to be nothing more than a corroded fuse holder. This was not uncommon in such a salty air climate as Key West. There also was bodywork to be done, which included patching the bottom of both doors with an aluminum strip that I made from salvaged aluminum from the navy salvage yard. The car got a spanking new black paint job with white stripping, new tires and sealed beam headlights, which were really a plus for night driving. I reupholstered some of the interior using blackout curtains left over from World War II. I was proud of my handiwork, and the Chevy looked and ran great. Rose was very patient during these eight months, for many a weekend she was alone at our apartment.

Preparations for our baby daughter included purchasing a folding car bed, a baby bottle warmer, which you plugged into the cigar lighter, (this later burned out after about the third use), an ice chest for her milk, a single burner hotplate on which to sterilize the baby bottles to make our daughter's formula, and a gas heater for the car to keep her and Rose and me warm. People in Key West thought I was nuts when I started asking dealers for a car heater; I eventually found a new South Wind Gas heater which I installed with minimal instructions. Later in the trip, the lack of proper installation of the heater posed somewhat of a problem. We also purchased a luggage carrier, with canvas cover, to put on the top of the car. All of this equipment, including the car parts, was purchased from good ol' Montgomery

Ward and Company. To make the luggage carrier waterproof I talked a Boatswains Mate First Class, named Neighbors, into making a canvas liner for the carrier. This along with the purchased cover proved to be very worthwhile, as it kept our entire luggage dry during the trip.

My daydreaming of all these accomplishments ended abruptly when I realized it was 1600 (4:00 PM) and time to pick up my leave papers and head for home to pick up Rose and Linda and hit the road. We lived several miles out of town in a development named Poinciana. It was a wartime housing project and consisted of several rows of two room efficiency apartments. The emphasis is on efficiency, because they were so small that if you ran in the front door too fast you would be out the back door before you could stop. There was a development just before we were to leave that posed a problem. For months, I had been trying to get Navy housing at the local seaplane base with no luck. was informed, two days before we were to leave, that I could move in on a date during the period I would be on leave. I asked the Administrative Officer, LCDR Wise, to handle this for me, and he graciously agreed. I gave him power of attorney and rent for a month. I told him our neighbor would move our belongings, which were sparse, when the time came. That solved the problem.

Rose had everything ready when I got home. I had packed the luggage carrier earlier and all we had to do was put in the last minute things, diapers (the paper type named Chucks), Linda's formula, the ice chest, and drinking water. The only civilian clothes I owned at that time were Levis, and I changed into them; we were ready to get underway. It was 1700 (5:00 PM) when we rolled out of the development headed North for Idaho. We had about a hundred miles to cover before we hit mainland Florida: this portion was called the overseas highway, for there were many bridges to cross over the keys, the longest being the seven-mile bridge. The road was built during the war and was still a toll road. The loaded Chevy purred as we pulled out on US 1, and we were on our way.

Once we passed the Boca Chica Naval Air Station there was little or no traffic. The highway, with the ocean on both sides, was a black stretch of asphalt that seemingly was endless as it disappeared ahead into the darkness. On each side, one could see the whitecaps of the ocean. The Chevy had a radio and was tuned to western music, we sailed on through the night. We passed through the little town of Marathon with a rush of lights from the few businesses, and then on into the dark of the night again. The miles were slowly slipping behind us and eventually we reached the junction South of Homestead, Florida and turned West to what we had been told was called Alligator Alley. This was the highway, which crossed the lower peninsula of the state towards the gulf coast.

The road was a narrow two-lane one, and there were canals on each side with many alligators. The headlights would pick up their beady eyes occasionally, which gave one a spooky feeling, but kept you alert with your driving. Rose kept her eyes glued to the road and baby Linda in her car bed slept through it all. Tall palms lined the road on each side, and with the water on both sides and the narrow asphalt road stretching ahead into the darkness it gave one the feeling of crossing a causeway over an alligator filled moat to some unseen castle.

Alligator Alley slowly slipped behind us and the highway turned North as we neared the gulf coast. There were more little towns, just wide spaces in the road, but we pressed on trying to make as many miles as we could on this first leg of our trip. There were no motels in those days, places for travelers to stay were called tourist cabins or camps, and in some areas, they were few and far between. We continued to drive and I finally started to feel the effects, I was getting tired and knew we had to find a place for the rest of the night. The sign ahead read, Punta Gorda, and as we passed over the little bridge into the town I saw a sign on our right that read, "Tourists Cabins". The place looked deserted as I turned into the driveway and stopped in front of what I considered to be the office. There was a single light dimly burning by the front door. I got out and rather timidly knocked on the door; it was 1:00 AM and I dreaded waking up someone. The knock was answered by a woman in her night robe. I asked if she had a cabin for the night, and in what I considered a rather unpleasant voice she told me to take number nine and pay her in the morning. She slammed the door, but we had a place to sleep. We had been on the road 8 hours and had driven over 300 miles. We did not need to be rocked to sleep that night, but we were well on our way to Idaho.

Reveille came early the next morning, as it would for the rest of our trip. This was the beginning of our second day on the road. We had to get on the road as soon as we could. We found a café for breakfast and after feeding Linda and ourselves, we were once again headed North. We passed through St. Petersburg and Tampa, the two largest cities on the Gulf side of Florida, and at Brooksville we turned left and picked up US 19. We followed US 19 the rest of the day and crossed over into Georgia late in the afternoon. The weather had been perfect and we were making good time. Linda was doing well in her little car bed, but Rose was beginning to get what we called diaper knees. Each time Linda needed a change Rose had to get on her knees and lean over the back of her seat to take off the dirty one and put on a clean one. The paper diapers were way too large and rather a loose fit to say the least. Once the dirty diaper was off out the window it went. I guess that was why they called them "Chucks". I told Rose to be sure there is not a State Patrolman behind us as I did not want one of those on his windshield. This was before there were any thoughts about the environment, and today I am ashamed we did it.

After crossing into Georgia, it started to rain and it was time to start looking for a tourist cabin. We had made good time and a reasonably early stop was in order. The only place we could find to stay was called, "Rose Tourist Camp". The buildings were of brick, very nice, and I figured expensive. The cost for a night's stay was $5.00; that was expensive to me in those years, for we usually found one for $3.00 or $3.50 per night. We enjoyed the night there, and the extra cost was worth it. Once in the room we sneaked in the hotplate and Rose proceeded to make formula for Linda for the next day's travel. This became a daily chore for Rose, and some nights it would be eleven o'clock before we would be stopped for the night. I look back and wonder how I could have driven for twelve, fourteen or even sixteen hours some days without falling asleep at the wheel. Rose's duties were no less arduous with taking care of Linda's needs. Youth knows no bounds I guess. We had stopped for lunch and then supper at some unremembered café, this would be the case for our entire trip. The list of insignificant cafes and restaurants would fade with memory.

We slept well that night and with the coming of morning, our third day on the road, we started what became a daily routine. Get up, dress, take care of our little daughter, load the car, find a place to eat breakfast, and then out on the highway again. Rain or shine, we drove on, picking our route as I thought best. There were no freeways in those days, so I chose what I always thought would be the best way to go. This is where the trip starts to become a journey. I was going by dead reckoning, as they say in the navy. I poured over my maps thinking this is the best way to go to avoid mountains, snow or whatever. This procedure was fruitful, but it added many unnecessary miles to our trip. That is why I call it a journey, for we meandered across the country first North, then West then North, or whatever the best way seemed.

Once all the preparations were completed, we headed out of Thomasville via route US 84. During the night, the rain had stopped and it was a pretty day. We followed US 84 as far as Dothan, Alabama and then turned northwest on US 231; this route took us through Montgomery and then on to Birmingham. We were slowly leaving the lower country behind. It was a pleasant drive and we were enjoying the scenery; this was the first time Rose or I had been through the real south. Our daughter Linda was handling the journey quite well, only requiring real attention when she was wet or hungry. The folding baby bed we had purchased from Montgomery Ward was serving her very well. Our only problem so far, with providing her needs, was the failure of the baby bottle warmer, which we plugged into the cigar lighter for current to heat her milk. The element had burned out and so we turned to the gas heater I had installed to provide the needed heat. It took no time to heat the milk; we just set the bottle in front of the heater. We had to be careful for it could get too warm for our baby.

The hours passed by and soon, we arrived in Birmingham, where we connected with highway US 78. We continued on headed northwest toward some point where I could join up with highway US 30, but that was still a few days drive, and there would be several route changes before then, depending on my dead reckoning navigation. The next change of direction would be at Memphis, Tennessee, but the day was beginning to wane and it would be time to find another tourist camp for the night. I kept driving hoping to get to Memphis before darkness over took us, but the night enveloped us and then the gas heater started to lose its heat. It was at this time that I became concerned for the safety and comfort of our new baby. We needed heat in the car and it was getting colder each mile we traveled further north.

The hours ticked by. We stopped to eat somewhere along the road, but had found no place to stop for the night. It must have been sometime near 10:00 PM when at last we found a place to stop. The name of the town was MT. something or other, I have long forgotten, but it was cold. We checked into the cabin, and Rose smuggled in the hot plate and commenced preparing Linda's formula for the next day. I tackled the job of trying to fix the heater. It was after 11:00 PM and there I was with my head up under the dash looking for something, but I knew not what. Eventually I gave up and we went to bed. In spite of my problem, I went to sleep quickly. It had been a long day, many miles driven and I was exhausted. Rose was as tired as I was; she had a lot of work to do taking care of our baby. Day 3 had been a long one, with many more miles of our trip behind us.

Day 4 dawned and we greeted it with an early reveille. It had rained and then turned to sleet during the night. We conducted our usual routine and then hit the road again. It was cold and there was some frozen slush on the road. We were only a few miles southeast of Memphis, Tennessee, and the Mississippi river, we would cross it there and head west on US 70. The road was slick in some places and I was driving carefully, when the road suddenly went downhill and through an underpass. I applied the foot brakes, but nothing happened; the brake pedal would not depress. I applied all my weight to the pedal and at the last moment it broke loose and the brakes took effect, and we slowed to a stop. It took me a few minutes to settle down and I finally realized what had happened. The brakes on the 1935 Chevrolet were mechanical brakes, not hydraulic as they would be in later years, and the cable linkage had frozen from the slush thrown up from the road. I tried the brake pedal and it was free, but I had too much slack in the cables and the brakes did not fully apply. I diagnosed the cause of this problem. It was the extra pressure I had to apply, to free the frozen brake cables. I had stretched them. I would have to be very careful driving until I could get the brakes adjusted properly. I had no idea where I would be able to have this done.

I now had two things to think of as we drove through Memphis, the heater and the brakes. The bridge across the Mississippi river at last appeared up ahead and we crossed over into the state of Arkansas. The weather cleared as we drove further west and I had adjusted myself to the decreased efficiency of the brakes. We settled down and began to enjoy the sunshine. I do not recall how far we had driven when Rose asked, "did it ever snow in Arkansas"? We had not driven five miles when out of nowhere a blinding snowstorm descended on us. The flakes were as big as a quarter and very wet. The vacuum powered windshield wipers on the Chevy could not clear the windshield. I would get out and clear the slush off by hand, but before I got back in the car, the wipers would become stuck again. This went on for about an hour and I was beginning to think we might have to give up on our trip if this kind of weather persisted. At this point, the storm stopped, and we were once again in sunshine and blue skies. I told Rose please do not speculate on the weather anymore.

The slightly warmer weather helped as the heater was putting out a little more heat, but still not up to par. The day was passing quickly and we changed to route US 64, which would take us through Tulsa, At Little Rock we made this change. I had started to think about where I could get the heater checked and repaired if necessary. I remembered that when I bought the heater I had received a book that listed authorized repair facilities. The next time we stopped for gas I got out the book. I found that Muskogee, Oklahoma was listed. That was a few more miles up the road, so I decided to stop there. We wrote down the address and had no trouble finding the garage once we arrived in town.

The garage was a small one and there was a café attached to the side of the garage. I drove the car into the garage, the mechanic asked me what I needed and I explained my problem with the heater. He told me he would look at it, but first Rose and baby Linda would be taken into the café where it was warm. That was his first concern; with that gesture, I knew here was a fine man.

The mechanic proceeded to remove the heater and then checked it out thoroughly. He even installed a new spark plug just to make sure that was not the problem. He examined every detail and could not find any mechanical problems. Finally, he looked at the copper tubing that connected the heater to the car's carburetor; he had coiled it up and had put it on his workbench. He picked it up and said I think this is the problem it is too long. The original length of the tubing was about four feet. I figured that was the length you were supposed to use, and I installed it that way. He said it should not be over thirty inches long, bingo, it came to me in a flash; the tubing was too long to get the gas from the carburetor bowl to the heater, not enough vacuum. I think my face got red, when I told him those guys in Florida, who installed it did not know much about heaters. I had never revealed the fact that I was the mechanic who had done the work. The higher elevation in northern Mississippi had decreased the vacuum; at lower elevations at the beginning of our trip, the vacuum was sufficient enough for the heater to work. I thanked the mechanic, paid him the one dollar and fifty cents he had charged me, and after getting Rose and Linda back in the car we were once again on our way.

Once on the highway I put the metal to the pedal and tried to make up for the time we had lost at the garage. I had become so used to the way the brake pedal worked, that I never thought to have the mechanic in Muskogee adjust the brakes. That would have to wait for some place down the road. The weather continued to be nice and eventually the city of Tulsa came into view. It was here we would change directions to head due north towards Omaha, Nebraska; we would take US 75. It was getting late in the afternoon as we headed for Kansas, our next state to cross. The miles rolled by and at last the Kansas state line was crossed; it was time to find a nights lodging and end day four on the road. We only drove a few miles into Kansas when we entered the town of Independence; It was not a very large town in those days, but we found a tourist cabin and called it a day.

Day 5 dawned bright and crisp with no snow. We had been most fortunate that we had not encountered any except for the brief storm in Arkansas. We were up early as our routine required, and on the road soon after breakfast. The highway, US 75, was almost a straight shot to Omaha, Nebraska, where we would turn west on US 30. The scenery consisted mainly of vast acres of farmland, now dormant from the summer crop of grain. The road was a narrow, two lane one and straight as an arrow with very few turns, but when you did turn it was at right angles. There was no cutting across a farmer's acreage; the road turned only at the edge of a farmer's section. I found this out when I failed to slow down for these turns, and almost overshot some of them. We were making good progress and the miles slowly rolled by. We passed through Topeka, the largest city before Omaha, and continued on our way. By late morning we were approaching Omaha, I wanted to bypass the city, so I took a route to the west of the city, which took us by Father Flannigan's Boy's Town. We had heard and read of this school, so it was a nice experience to be able to pass by and see it.

We now knew that US 30 was only a few miles away. We would then turn west towards Idaho. Fremont, Nebraska was the town where we would hit US 30 and I decided it was time to stop and have the brakes adjusted. I had been putting this off far too long. I found a garage on the highway and pulled in to have the adjustment. While this was being taken care of I decided that I should buy a set of tire chains, in case we hit some snow further west, which in all probability would happen at this time of the year. It did not take long for the mechanic to take care of the brake situation and we were once again on our way. Rose and Linda were doing okay, except for Rose's knees, which hurt from having to change those diapers while kneeling on her seat and leaning over Linda's car bed.

We had stopped for lunch somewhere along the way, but we never paid much attention to where that was, just eating and getting back on the road was our main concern. Once on US 30 I realized we were headed south as well as west. This was one of those times when the trip became a journey. I was putting on extra miles and if I had turned west at Topeka, I could have saved us some miles of driving and joined US 30 further to the west. I was so intent on getting on US 30 that I did not study my map as well as I should. All I knew was that US 30 ran through my home town of Twin Falls and the sooner I got on it the better. The day was beginning to run out on us and I wanted to get off the road before darkness set in, so we drove as far as Grand Island, Nebraska and stopped for the night. I think the name of the tourist cabins was the "Black and White", for in later years while driving west from Norfolk, Virginia we stayed at this same place.

Once we checked in it was time to unload our nighttime necessities. We had to smuggle in the hot plate so we could prepare Linda's formula for the next day. Personal electric appliances were not allowed in the cabins, so we had to sneak the hotplate in unnoticed. The first thing we always looked for, when we rented a cabin for the night, was did it have an electrical outlet. Fortunately, the cabins always had one, so we never had to go back to the office and say we do not want this cabin. Poor Rose then had to sterilize the baby bottles, and make the formula; she had a lot of work to do after a long day's drive. We were both tired, but another day closer to our destination. Day 5 was behind us, the heater worked fine, and it was great to have brakes that responded when you pushed the pedal. The car had performed fine; I was proud of all the work I had done in the months prior to our trip. Most important was our baby was taking this long ride without any trouble; she was a good baby.

Every morning of our trip, so far, we were up and on the road before daylight. The task of getting ready to travel had become routine. One task that was annoying was draining the car radiator each night, so it would not freeze. This became important, for the further north we drove the more temperature dropped below zero. For reasons of economy, I had not spent money for anti-freeze for the car. I had started doing this once we passed Memphis.

Today was the beginning of day six, and with our predawn departure, we were many miles down the road when night time faded from the windshield and sunrise appeared in our rear view mirror. The towns of Kearney, North Platte, and Ogallala slipped by as the day wore on and we were getting ever closer to Wyoming and the beginning of the Rocky Mountains. There was no snow on the ground, and for that time of the year, it was amazing. It was cold but traveling so far had been without any weather borne mishaps. At last, we crossed into Wyoming and stopped in Cheyenne for gas. Soon we would start to climb and I was hoping I would not encounter snow and have to put on the new chains I had bought in Fremont.

Today highway I-80 crosses Wyoming and bypasses many of the old US 30 sections, but such was not the case in our journey. The highway from Cheyenne to Laramie followed old US 30. On this stretch of road, we encountered our first bit of construction, and the highway was rough. I noticed that my gas gauge level was slowly dropping; I could not figure why. I had filled up in Cheyenne, but by the time we arrived in Laramie the tank was half-empty. I stopped at a service station and filled up again; after filling the tank, I lifted the hood to check the engine and found that one of the spark plug wires had come loose. This undoubtedly was the cause of the increased fuel consumption; I had not noticed any difference in the way the engine ran. I figured that because of the rough road I had been unaware of it. I connected the loose wire and started the engine, all seemed to be okay. We were on our way again.

It was late afternoon and I had planned to drive as far as Rock Springs, Wyoming, still many miles down the road. Leaving Laramie, we started climbing passing through Bosler, Rock River, Medicine Bow, and at last, we arrived in Rawlins. Our planned stop for the night was the next town of any size, and it was now dark. The sun had set some hours back, but we had to press on. The temperature had really dropped and I did not have a heavy jacket. I had been wearing a light ski jacket, but that did not keep out the cold. There was a little snow on the ground, but the roads were clear.

I do not recall how far it was after we left Rawlins when Rose and I noticed lights on the right side of the road pointing up into the air. They were off the road in the sagebrush. I slowed down as we approached the site and then stopped when I saw that it was a car. I got out, took my flashlight and headed to the area; it was a wreck and the car was upside down. The lights were still on and the front wheels were still turning. Apparently this had just happened, although there had been no traffic passing us in hours. I slowly approached the car with grave apprehension, for I had no idea what kind of carnage I might encounter.

I called out and asked if there was someone there, there was no answer. I gingerly stepped all around the car, no one. I searched the surrounding area, continuing to call. I had goose bumps all over my body, some from the cold others from either fear or anxiety. I looked at those front wheels, now slowing but still revolving. This was a real mystery. What happened and where were the occupants? The cold had really gotten to me and shivering I hurried back to our car and got in telling Rose that I could find no one in or around the wreck. Still confused I started the car and drove away towards Rock Springs; I had to report this to some authorities.

Rock Springs finally came into view and the faint glare of those city lights shining in the distance was a most welcome sight. We drove down the main street, spotted a tourist camp named "Rose's Cabins" and turned it for the night. The room had an attached garage for the car; there was no door on it but at least the car was under a roof. I drained the engine once we had checked in and we settled in for some rest. It had been a very long day with a couple of interesting occurrences. I did call the local authorities and reported the wreck and the circumstances, as I knew them. The police did not seem too concerned, so we went to bed.

It was pitch black when we arose the next morning, and it was cold, minus 15 degrees. As usual, we followed our morning routine for getting ready to travel; this was day seven and it had been a week since we left Key West. Long hours on the road made one day blend into another; time seemed to stand still as your mind became dulled by the rigors of travel. I filled the car radiator with warm water and we were on our way. I hoped we would be able to make it all the way to Twin Falls today; it would be a long drive.

There was no traffic on the road as we pulled out of Rock Springs. The few lights shining in town soon disappeared behind us, and we were out in the open desert. We had driven perhaps about twenty miles when the engine began to miss and slow down. My heart seemed to jump up into my throat; all I could think of was becoming stalled out there in the cold with a young baby. Rose and I in unison were coaxing the car over every little rise in the highway. We sat on our seats and unconsciously tried to move it with body motion. I kept straining looking ahead for some building or service station, but there was nothing but open desert and sagebrush. I knew the next place on the highway where we might get help was called "Little America", but I was not sure how far that was. The miles were now flowing by very slowly and the strain on me was beginning to tell. I was frightened and I had no idea how long the car would continue to run. After what seemed hours, the outline of the buildings at "Little America" appeared on the horizon, with God's help we were going to make it.

Little America was aptly named for it was isolated and very cold, like Antarctica. I pulled up to what I assumed was the garage and noticed it was an underground building. The mechanic opened the doors and we drove down into a warm, steam heated work area. I told the mechanic about the car, but before he started to look at the engine he insisted Rose and Linda be moved into the warmer office. Here was another man, like the one in Muskogee, who thought of my families comfort and safety before he tackled the job at hand.

It did not take him long to find the problem; the distributor condenser had failed, so electrical current to the spark plugs was insufficient for the engine to run properly. I had been very lucky to drive as far as I did under this condition. I told the mechanic that I had put new points and condenser in before we left on our trip, but when the plug wire came loose, he said that caused the condenser to fail. He installed a new condenser, adjusted the carburetor for the higher elevation, and took the car out for a test drive. He said you should have no more problems. He only charged me $3.50; I have never forgotten that kind and generous mechanic.

We rolled out of the garage feeling relieved that the problem was not severe, now we had to make up for lost time. Our route took us west through Evanston, Wyoming and then into Utah. We bypassed Salt Lake City and turned northwest through Ogden. The afternoon had run its course and darkness was not far ahead. I turned the car toward Tremonton, Utah headed north towards Burley, Idaho. The highway was high desert country. I was familiar with this stretch, as I hitch hiked this route, on my way home from Salt Lake City, when I was trying to enlist in the navy. There were no cars on the road and I was making good time; I was driving at top speed for a thirteen-year old car. The miles were flowing behind us and I was sure we would make it to Twin Falls.

Somewhere between Snowville and Burley, I heard a whirring sound and looked down at the dashboard, where the noise seemed to emanate. The hand on the speedometer was going back and forth and the odometer wheels were jumping. I knew I had to do something about that or the whole unit would be ruined. It was far too cold to get out and under the car to disconnect the cable, so I took it loose up under the dash where it attached to the speedometer. I tucked the loosened end of the cable up amongst some wiring and figured it would stay there until we got to Twin Falls. That proved to be a wrong assumption; we had only driven a few miles when the cable came loose and started whipping back and forth between my legs. This presented a scary situation, for I was not sure what part of my anatomy might become entangled with that cable. I decided to gamble and we drove on keeping a close watch on that whipping cable. Rose and I had a good laugh on what might happen.

The desert finally faded behind us and we passed through the town of Burley, Twin Falls was only thirty miles away. It was almost midnight when we pulled into the driveway of my folk's home. They were awake and let us into the garage. My dad had sold his car during the war and so the garage was empty. After all the greetings and moving some of our belongings into the house, I drained the radiator of the car. We had made it with a minimum of difficulties. We would rest here a bit before driving on to Kellogg, Idaho, Rose's home. Christmas was just a few days away, and I had just celebrated my twenty-sixth birthday.

Shortly after our arrival in Twin Falls, I removed the speedometer and took it to a repair shop. They rebuilt it and only charged me $6.00; the rebuilt one worked like new. At the same time, I told the shop about an oil leak around the distributor shaft. I had removed the distributor and made a new gasket, but the leak persisted. The mechanic removed it and cleaned a small drain hole in the housing, which allowed the oil to drain back to the crankcase instead of leaking around the shaft. He said this was a common problem; I had not seen the drain hole when I had worked on the leak. He did not charge me for this repair. I could never forget how well, economically, I had fared for repairs on this trip.

We spent a week at my folk's home, which included Christmas Day, and a side trip to Hailey, Idaho. I had lived in Hailey and gone to school there at various times, and my step-relatives lived there. We had a nice visit, I did some skiing and we bought a baby bed at Model's store for Linda. Back in Key West we had been using a crib for Linda that a shipmate had loaned us. I did not have room in the car or on top in the luggage carrier for the bed, so we shipped it to Key West by Greyhound Bus. As I recall it only cost us $5.00 to ship it. At the end of our seven days it was time to get on the road again, this time we would drive to northern Idaho to Kellogg and Wardner, where Rose grew up as a child.

A few days after Christmas we loaded the car and headed for northern Idaho. As usual our departure was in the early morning hours. We headed west on US 30 and followed it as far as Boise where we turned north on State Highway 55. The road slowly climbed as we passed through the towns of Horse Shoe Bend, Smith's Ferry, Cascade, and McCall. At McCall we turned west for a few miles to join up with US 95 at New Meadows. The highways thus far had been mostly dry. The day wore on and we were enjoying the scenery, there was snow on the mountains, but the roads were dry. Neither Rose nor I had traveled this area before, so this was a new experience. At New Meadows we turned north and followed the Salmon river through the little town of Riggins and then on to White Bird.

At White Bird I stopped to fill up with gas. The service station was located at the north end of the little town, as I stood there filling the tank I looked up and I could see White Bird hill. The road started to climb as soon as you left town. I had heard about the hill and how it winded back and forth, ever climbing for about twelve miles. The road was constructed mainly on a south facing ridge, which gave it exposure to the south, and the sun. This could be a plus if the snow got deep, there might be some chance of thawing. I put the gas cap on and climbed into the car, and we headed up the hill. The roads in those days were narrow and with all the twists and turns going up the hill it was a challenge. I was glad when we finally crested the summit. We soon passed through Grangeville; I knew our next stop for the night would have to be Lewiston, Idaho. It was still too far to Kellogg to drive in one day.

We finally left the high land and started downhill to Lewiston. The closer we got to Lewiston the warmer the weather, and it felt good. Lewiston's elevation is about 750 feet above sea level, and the climate is usually quite mild. We drove through town and found a nice place to stay for the night. It was so nice to be able to get out of the car and walk around with just a light jacket, especially in December. We had a long drive behind us and the tourist cabin was a welcome sight. We unloaded our necessities and settled in for the night. Little baby Linda was doing fine; she had handled the trip very well with only the usual demands of being fed and changed. With a good night's rest we should make Kellogg tomorrow.

The weather in Lewiston continued to be mild, and during the night there was a light rain. We awoke to what seemed to be almost like a spring day, but it was still December. With good luck we should arrive in Kellogg. We loaded the car, ate breakfast and once again we were on our way. White Bird hill had been a good climb, and Lewiston hill was another one we had to conquer. To reach the crest of this hill was a shorter distance, but it was a steeper climb. The mild temperature of the valley quickly faded away and once we reached the top we were back in the world of winter. There was snow on the ground, but the roads were passable, although there were icy spots, which made you pay attention to your driving.

We passed through the town of Moscow, where the University of Idaho was located, and continued on to the little town of Potlatch. We had been following US 95, which would take us through the city of Coeur d' Alene where we would turn east on US 10 for Kellogg. I had studied my map and noticed that Alternate US 95 turned at Potlatch and would join US 10 east of Coeur d' Alene. This appeared to me to be a shorter route to Kellogg. I decided to follow that road, which turned out to be a rather hairy drive. This route ran along the east side of Lake Coeur d' Alene and it was winding and ice covered. There were evergreen trees on both sides of the highway, so the sun never got a chance to melt the snow. Several times I thought I should put the chains on the tires, but figured they would not be much help on the ice, I drove slowly and finally we intersected US 10. The highway, from this point on to Kellogg, ran along the hillside, winding in and out of the trees, but eventually we emerged from the forest and entered Silver Valley. This was the home of the Bunker Hill mine; the biggest silver, zinc and lead mine in the world. We had reached the outskirts of Kellogg. We drove to Rose's brother's house and was warmly greeted by him and his family. We had at last reached the northern terminus of our journey from Key West.

Mitch and Mildred, Rose's brother and his wife, had two young boys, Gary and Dale, and their house was very small, so Rose and I were invited to stay with her two sisters, Mary and Mildred in their little apartment. During our stay in Kellogg I got the chance to get acquainted with Rose's family; this was the first time we really had time for this. I had only been with them on one other occasion and that was under sad circumstances and for a short period of time. Rose's mother had passed away a year earlier and we had come home for the funeral.

My leave from the navy was for thirty days and most of it had been expended traveling. We stayed in Kellogg about a week, which included New Year's eve. Rose and I went to the Sunshine Inn with her sister Mary for the evening's entertainment. Mary's boyfriend, Del Linhart, was working as a bartender there. Rose and I spent the evening dancing and having a good time. Rose's sister, Mildred was babysitting our baby daughter. Her boyfriend, Bob Berquist, was away in the navy. During the course of the evening Rose and I won two jackpots in the dime slot machine, which helped replenish our dwindling cash supply.

A day or two before New Year's I realized we did not have enough of my leave time left to make it back to Key West on time. The only choice I had was request an extension of my leave or be AOL (absent over leave). I drafted a telegram to my command and told them there was a lot of snow on the ground, I was too far from Key West to make it back on time, that I was having a good time, and could I have a ten day extension. I think I had them over a barrel; I had enough unused leave on the books, so they granted my wish.

It was time to leave and head back to Key West; we had enjoyed our visit and had been able to proudly show off our new baby daughter. All good things must come to an end, so the day after New Year's we headed south. This time I took US 10 to Coeur d' Alene and took the main US 95 highway south. I was not going to travel the alternate route we took on our arrival; it was far to winding and icy. This turned out to be a proper decision, and we arrived in Moscow, Idaho in a matter of a few hours. We had decided to stop for a short visit with an old shipmate of mine, who was going to the University of Idaho.

Dare Kibble and I met on the train when we were on our way to Salt Lake City to enlist in the navy back in 1940. Dare lived in Boise and I had known of him when I attended Borah High School there. Dare was in the high school ROTC, and I had remembered seeing him in uniform. I introduced myself and we became friends. We went through boot camp together, machinist's mate school in Norfolk, Virginia and we were assigned to the USS Tangier AV8. Three weeks before the Japanese attack on Pearl Harbor, he was transferred to Wake Island, where he was later captured when Wake fell. Our ship was in Pearl Harbor when he got his orders to be transferred. I had not seen him since his release as a prisoner of war. I had gotten his address in Moscow from his mother who lived in Boise, when we had passed through on our way to Kellogg.

We found Dare's house with no trouble. He was surprised when I knocked and he came to the door. He had married and had a baby daughter. His wife's name was Ann, and he introduced her to Rose and me. We spent a couple of hours bringing each other up-to-date on the years we had been apart. He did not relate very much of his experiences as a prisoner of the Japanese, and I did not press him for details. He had suffered physically and had suffered from beriberi. He was going to the University under the GI Bill and majoring in accounting and business as I recall. Our visit was far too short, but time was of essence to Rose and I, we had to get going as there were only about ten days left of my leave. We said our farewells and departed.

It was mid-afternoon when we left, and we had decided to spend the night in Lewiston at the same tourist cabins we patronized on our way to Kellogg. As we descended Lewiston Hill, the temperature became warmer, because of the lower elevation. It was nice and balmy and once again, we enjoyed walking around without having to wear heavier clothing. We knew that tomorrow we would be climbing up to higher elevations and it would be colder. We had stopped early enough to take care of our daily chores without having to hurry. We knew from here on it would be a tight schedule and there would be many long hours each day on the road.

Early the next morning we were up and on our way before daylight. The road was still bare and dry, but as we started to climb towards Grangeville, we began to get back to snow country. We descended White Bird Hill and on through Riggins toward New Meadows where we left US 95 and joined State Highway 55. The snow became deeper, but the road was passable with careful driving. After leaving McCall, we ran into frozen slush on the road, and I debated whether to stop and put on my chains. The road was not slick, just bumpy from the frozen slush, so I slowed down and pressed on. We stopped in Cascade to eat; little Linda was sleeping in her car bed, so we parked in the sun and left her to her baby dreams. We could see the car from the café, so we knew she was all right.

The icy road continued for about one hundred miles, but eventually we left it behind and started to descend to warmer weather. There would be no stopping until we got to my folk's home in Twin Falls, except to buy gas for the car. Boise finally came into view and we passed through heading east on US 30. Mountain Home slipped by and disappeared in the rear view mirror, as did all the other little towns along the way. The car was running fine and we kept going. We arrived in Twin Falls late at night; my folks were expecting us. I parked in the garage, drained the water from the radiator and we went to bed. There would be no dallying tomorrow as we had to keep moving.

It was another early rising, and the beginning of the long journey back to Key West. We completed our preparations and then said good-bye to my folks. My planned route would take us to the south and across all the southern western states. We headed south from Twin Falls on

US 93. There would be a lot of sagebrush-covered land on this route, but I figured we would stay clear of the snow and higher elevations. I had traveled the road from Twin Falls to Wells a couple of times, but that was back during the war. I had been able to come home on leave twice for a short time and had made the trip by Greyhound Bus. The road had not changed and this short section of highway brought back distant memories. At Wells, Nevada we turned east on US 40 and followed it to Wendover, Utah. I did not want to drive through Salt Lake City, so I turned southeast on a secondary road some miles east of Wendover and connected with US 91 at American Forks, Utah. The scenery changed from sagebrush to farmland, as we got closer to American Forks.

The weather had been cold but no snow or rain; at American Forks, we started to run into sleet. I had not paid enough attention to my map and did not realize that US 91 ran parallel to the southern part of the Rockies, which was high country. The sleet and rain persisted most of the day. In spite of my circuitous route, we were making good time. The day wore on and as nighttime fell, so we stopped for the night. I do not remember the name of the town, one of the few I have forgotten as I have been able to recall all the others where we stayed. Once again we were back to our on the road routine; first we smuggled in the hot plate and then our belongings. Rose then began her chore of sterilizing Linda's baby bottles and then making her formula for the next day. I continued to drain the radiator in the car each night, for we were still having below freezing temperatures. Day one of our homeward bound journey came to a close, and we turned in for the night.

Day 2 began as usual and we were on our way before daylight. There had been relatively light traffic ever since we left Twin Falls. Most of the cars we encountered were near towns, once we left the towns behind the traffic diminished. The day wore on as we passed numerous little towns. The larger cities we encountered were Spanish Fork, Cedar City, and St. George. We stopped only for gas and a bite to eat; I had to cover as many miles as possible, for there was no margin for any delays. The extension of my leave was slowly but surely running out; I only had eight days left in which to get back to Key West. Rose and Linda were doing fine and in spite of the long hours of driving, I seemed to be holding up okay.

It was starting to get dark when we left St. George, Utah; the Nevada state line was not too far distant. I had hoped to make it to Las Vegas, but realized that was just a bit too far this day. My eyes were getting heavy and it was time to start looking for some tourist cabins for the night. I think the radio music was the one thing that kept me awake and concentrating on my driving. The desert ahead was dark with no encouraging light from some little town where we might stop for the night. Time seemed to stand still, but at last, a faint glimmer in the distance raised my hopes, maybe there was a place we could stay. That faint glimmer finally appeared and the little wide spot in the road named Glendale, Nevada came into view. There were cabins there, and at last, we had a place to sleep for the night. I pulled in and registered at the office, parked the car and then the routine of preparations for our daughter for the next day's travel began. Rose deserved a medal for all of her hard work each night after a hard days travel. Needless to say, we slept soundly.

Day three of our journey started with the usual preparations for the day. It was still dark when we pulled out on the highway and headed south. Slowly the mountains of Utah fell behind and we crossed over the Nevada state line and descended into the valley and the city of Las Vegas. Las Vegas in those days was an unimposing town in the desert. The city of Reno was the big deal, known as the "Biggest Little City in the World". Our passage through Las Vegas was uneventful and we continued on US 95. As we got closer to the town of Boulder City, we started seeing signs informing us of Boulder Dam (Hoover Dam today). I told Rose that we should drive by and see it as long as we were this close. We really did not have that much time to spare, but we decided we might never get another chance so we turned off and drove to the dam.

The road down to the dam was narrow and winding, fortunately we were the only car on the road. Our first glimpse of the dam was very impressive and we were glad we were taking the time to see it. We drove out to the middle of the dam and parked, and got out and looked over the side. The construction of the bridge was one of the greatest achievements of the century at that time. I took a picture of our parked car as a memento of our visit. Taking one last look, we then climbed in the car and started our winding way back to US 95. By this time, daylight had been with us for several hours, and we were a bit behind schedule as we headed ever south into the vast desert of Nevada.

The two-lane road stretched ahead of us in what seemed to be an unbroken straight line as far as the eye could see. It was a never ending rolling road, up and down, up and down, and we got a thrill from riding it like a roller coaster. The front shock absorbers on the Chevy were hydraulic, which gave the car a front and back swaying motion whenever we crested one of the little hills. This was our amusement as we let the long miles roll away behind us. We passed through the town of Searchlight, Nevada and soon after crossed the state line into California. At Needles, California we joined US 66 for short distance to the east and then on again on US 95. At Vidal, California we turned east off US 95 toward the wide spot in the road called Earp. I stopped there and bought five cigars in a saloon, which turned out to be a fiasco. I lighted one of the cigars, it had dried up so much from the heat and low humidity of the desert that it flared out like a head of lettuce. I almost singed my eyebrows, but I smoked every one of them along the way. I was not about to waste the money they had cost me.

Leaving Earp, we crossed the Colorado River into the state of Arizona and through what is known now as the town of Parker. I am not sure Parker existed then, as I do not remember it. We followed Arizona state highway 95 for a short distance and then turned east on state road 72. This was dry country; it looked as if it had never seen rain. The temperature now was in the high 80s and a tailwind had developed, which began to cause a problem. The car's engine overheated and at the junction of state road 72 and US 60 steam started to rise from under the hood. This spot in the desert was called

Hope, and I could see why. There were two houses and nothing else. I pulled off the road, stopped and lifted the hood to check the radiator. When I rebuilt the engine I had put in a new radiator, so I was pretty sure it was not that, it had to be lack of water. I made the mistake, big one, of loosening the radiator cap and the hot water blew out and was gone. I should have waited until the engine had cooled, now where was I going to get water in this godforsaken spot in the desert. I walked to one of the nearby houses and knocked on the door, but no one answered. I went back to the car and told Rose our problem.

Rose had taken a half-gallon fruit jar with us when we left Key West, in which she carried water for our daughter. It was about half full and that was all the water we had. We sat there until the engine cooled and then I put that pitiful bit of water in the radiator and we started on our way again. Every few miles I would stop and let the engine cool, then we would repeat this procedure, constantly scanning the countryside for a source of water, but to no avail. The afternoon seemed endless, but at last, we arrived at the town of Wickenburg, Arizona. I pulled into a gas station, filled up with water and gas, and thanked our lucky stars that we had made it. My ignorance of desert driving almost caused a tragedy; I should have known the importance of carrying an ample supply of water with us.

My nerves finally began to settle down and we headed out on US 60 toward Phoenix, Arizona. The day was rapidly drawing to a close and daylight would be gone in a few hours. Fortunately, the engine had not been damaged by the overheating, so we were able to continue on our journey, hopefully with all problems behind us. The next town on our route was Glendale, Arizona, located a few miles north of Phoenix. This is where we stopped for the night. It had been a very long and eventful day; we thanked our lucky stars it had turned out in our favor. Day 3 was behind us; we had covered many miles and we still had many more to go. In spite of this, we slept well.

The raucous sound of an alarm clock in the early pre-dawn hours has never aroused my enthusiasm for getting out of bed. The only times I accepted that noise was when I was going hunting or fishing, but this morning it was urgent that we get up and on the road. The first three days we had been heading due south, now it was time we start closing the distance between Key West and us; we had to turn east, which we would do once we got to Phoenix, Arizona.

Glendale, where we had spent the night, was only a short distance northwest of Phoenix. It only took us about an hour to reach the downtown area. We stopped at a café for breakfast, which had been our custom on the trip. We would get up early, drive a while and then find a convenient place along the way to eat. Once breakfast was consumed, we were on our way. Phoenix was not an exceptionally big city at the time, so we followed US 60 through town and headed for Globe, Arizona. This put us up in the mountains again for a short while. At Globe we turned southeast on US 70, which would take us on into the state of New Mexico. The scenery since we left Twin Falls had been entirely desert, except for the short time we had driven in Utah, and it continued to be the same.

There were a few small towns along the way, but the driving was monotonous. The one consolation was the weather; it had been warm during the days ever since we left Las Vegas. At last, we crossed the state line and entered New Mexico. The first town we passed through was Lordsburg; at our present rate of travel, I was hoping we would be able to make El Paso, Texas by nightfall. The highway ran parallel to the railroad and for miles it followed this right of way, but we never saw a train. We were alone and for miles there was nothing to see but more desert.

We had driven several miles from Lordsburg when a loud rattling sound was heard from under the engine hood. Our blissful tranquility was suddenly shattered by this ominous noise. I turned off the engine and coasted to a stop on the shoulder of the highway. I had no idea what may have caused this noise and was apprehensive about even looking under the hood. My first thought after I collected my senses was the water pump fan might have come off and hit the radiator. If that were the case, we were in big trouble. I got out and slowly lifted the hood; my first glance was at the radiator and water pump fan. They were intact.

I walked around to the other side of the car and raised the hood on that side, and the first thing I saw was the generator, the belt pulley had parted in the center. The pulley was cast in two parts, when riveted together they formed a pulley. The rivets had failed and the two sections had parted, so the pulley belt could not drive the generator. The loose halves were what caused the noise. I related this problem to Rose and told her not to worry, as I had a coffee can of screws and rivets in the trunk of the car. I had brought them along for such an emergency as this. I found a big boulder by the roadside and moved it over to use as my anvil when I riveted the pulley back together. I opened the trunk and got out my can of rivets, except there were no rivets. I had picked up the wrong coffee can when I packed for the trip, instead of rivets and screws there were miscellaneous items of wire. Rose did not take this news too readily, but I told her I thought I might be able to use the old rivets and hope it could get us into Deming, New Mexico, which was the next town down the line.

Fortunately the severed rivets had remained in one half of the pulley, but there was not much metal sticking through when I put the halves back together for me to peen over and thus hold the pulley together. I was able to affect a repair, but I knew it would not last all the way to Key West. The best I could hope for was that it would hold until we got to Deming or by some good luck, there might be a garage along the way where I could get it fixed properly. I put my tools and the coffee can with the wire back in the trunk. I cussed myself for not checking the contents of the can before we left home. I had been in too big of a hurry to get started on our trip.

I climbed back in the car, crossed my fingers and pressed the starter. The engine started and there was no noise. Slowly we drove back onto the highway and started praying our way to Deming. We had driven several miles and I was constantly looking for a garage or someplace where I could get some parts or rivets. To our surprise, there appeared a weather beaten sign up ahead that advertised a blacksmith shop with an arrow pointing over the railroad tracks. I strained my neck and sure enough there I could see the top of a small building. I turned left over the tracks and pulled up to the shop. There was no sign of any activity or any person around, but an older man slowly came out. I hastily told him my problem and asked him if he had some rivets I could bye. He told me no he did not have any rivets, and I thought a blacksmith's shop without some rivets; this guy has to be kidding, he was not. He said he did have a brand new electric welder and he could weld the pulley for me.

It did not take me long to get the generator off and the pulley removed. He took it from me and disappeared behind a piece of canvas hanging from the ceiling that separated me from the welding area. In no time, sparks started to fly and smoke started pouring out from behind the canvas. I thought boy, in a few minutes I will have it repaired and then on our way again. The sparks and smoke continued, I thought what is he doing. He soon answered my question when he appeared from behind the curtain and handed me the hot pulley. The guy had filled the entire pulley groove with weld; the fan belt could not fit where it should. I explained this to him, but he was unruffled and told me he had a brand new portable grinder and I could grind off the excess weld. It took me the better part of an hour to do this and I wore out the grinding wheel, the result was a very rough surface in the pulley groove. I knew the fan belt would not last long running over such a rough surface. I bit my tongue to withhold what I wanted to tell him, paid him and we were on our way.

Once again, we had wasted precious time and we were behind schedule. I knew we could not make it to El Paso. Our best hope was to get to Deming and find a cabin for the night. It was dark when we arrived in Deming, but there was some tourist cabins located on the main street. We checked in and settled in for the night. Tomorrow I would have to see if there was a Chevrolet garage in town, and pray they had a new pulley. The other alterative would be an entire new generator, and the old pocket book might not be able to handle that expense. Day 4 had presented its surprises; I hoped the rest of the trip would be less eventful. I worried myself to sleep that night.

There was no need for an alarm clock this morning; I awoke with the thought still on my mind of finding a pulley for the car generator. We would not be on the road early today, we had to wait until eight o'clock for the stores to open for business. I do not recall how I found where the Chevy garage was located, but it turned out to be just up the block from where we spent the night. It was cold out and my light jacket did not warm me much as I headed up the street. The Chevy agency was just a hole in the wall place, and I did not have much hope of finding what I needed as I entered the building. I told the man behind the counter what I needed, and to my surprise, he had one in stock. I paid for the new pulley, and clutched it in my hand as if it were pure gold as I went back to the tourist cabin.

It did not take me long to take the generator off the engine; I was getting quite adept at that. While I was working, I kept thanking my lucky stars for being able to get a new pulley. My hands were numb from the cold, but I never seemed to notice, all that was important was getting the engine running again and get on the road. I put in the last bolt, adjusted the tension on the fan belt, closed the hood and told Rose we were ready to go. I had no idea how far we would be able to drive today since we had several hours to make up because of our late start.

Once again, it was more desert to cross; it seemed it would never end. The first town after Deming was Las Cruces and a short time later we crossed the Texas state line. El Paso was the next city and it was not much in those days. The highway ran through the center of town, today the freeway runs north of the old city. We continued to follow US 90 as it disappeared over the horizon to the east. Traffic was still very light and we had the desert all to ourselves, the monotony was broken only by the music on the radio. Our daughter, Linda, bless her heart had been a good baby through all of the mishaps. She seemed to be thriving and growing bigger every day. Rose seemed to be doing okay except for her diaper knees; it would be interesting to know how many times she had kneeled over the back seat to change Linda.

The miles rolled by and at last, we arrived at Van Horn, Texas; here we turned southeast towards Del Rio, still following US 90. This was a roundabout way to cross Texas, but there were no freeways in 1948. The towns were few and far between, and in the back of my mind, I kept thinking that this is no place to have any problems. In those days roads or highways were built to connect towns so they wandered from place to place If one needed help it might be a long time in arriving. Del Rio finally came into view and I remember seeing the huge radio tower of the broadcasting station. Del Rio was one of the powerful radio stations that broadcasted county western music, which could be received all across the country. I used to listen to the station in Key West when I stood long night watches at the naval command where I was assigned. It was interesting to be able to see the source of the broadcasts. The tall towers soon faded from view as we continued on east. San Antonio was where I wanted to spend the night, but I knew we could not make it. The day was ending and darkness was approaching. We finally decided to stop when we entered Uvalde, Texas. All I remember now is we slept there, the town or where we ate are long forgotten. Day 5 had been a good one, a long one, but at least without any problems. We still had half a continent to cross before my leave expired. The coming days would be extra long.

Each day we traveled made getting up early in the morning more difficult. The long hours behind the steering wheel were catching up on me, so when day six dawned I could have slept until noon, but we had to keep going. I had no idea how far we would travel this day, but once on the road I knew it would be after dark before we stopped for the night. I had just a few days left of my leave to get back to Key West. This was the thought on my mind as we pulled out on US 90 and continued east.

Slowly but surely we were leaving the desert behind us; that was a welcome change of scenery. Ranches and farmland began to dot the countryside and there were more green fields to see. The next big city would be San Antonio, it would be great to be able to stop and visit the Alamo, but that was out of the question. On our way into town we passed Kelly Field, this was a US Army Air Force Base. The month before I joined the Navy in 1940 my favorite teacher in high school, Florence M. Rees, had stopped here and gathered some information on the pilot flight program. She had done this for me and was going to tell me of the program when she returned from her trip. She told me not to join the Navy until she had talked to me. By the time her telegram had arrived, I had already enlisted. There were memories connected to that base.

San Antonio faded behind us and we pressed on toward Houston. There were small towns along the way, but Houston was the next big city. Rain started to fall near Houston and it would follow us for quite some distance. The miles seemed to flow by so slowly, and I was driving as fast as the law would allow. The rain had slowed us down a bit and finally it stopped. Houston was now some miles behind us. Darkness had overtaken us when we approached Beaumont, Texas. By this time I could hardly hold my eyes open; I told Rose I was going to pull off the road and rest a bit. The shoulder of the road was wide and grassy, so I slowed down and pulled off in a wide spot. As soon as we drove on the grass all four wheels sank to the hubs of the wheels. The rain had made a bog of the shoulder, which I could not perceive because it was too late. I gunned the engine to try and pull free of the mud, but that did not work. We were stuck and there had been no traffic going or coming for some time. I looked around but there were no buildings in the area.

As I was standing on the road trying to evaluate our situation a set of headlights appeared on the highway coming our way. I stepped out on the asphalt and started waving my arms frantically hoping the driver would see me and stop. The driver started past me then stopped and backed up. He was driving an International pickup truck I will never forget. He rolled down his window and I asked him if he could pull me out of the mud. I told him I did not know the grass was so wet with mud underneath when I had driven off the road to rest. He told me he would be glad to help, but he did not have anything to hook on to me to get me out. I told him I had a set of tire snow chains in my trunk and we could tie them together. He told me okay and that is how we got back on the road. I offered to pay him but he said no, he was glad to do it. I did not argue with him, as our cash situation was not in that good of shape.

This bit of diversion shook all the tiredness out of me, I was now wide awake and ready to drive some more. We continued on past Beaumont and at last crossed the Louisiana state line. The huge state of Texas was at last behind us. I felt relief that we had made it in a 1935 Chevrolet, and proud that my overhaul had paid off. In a small town somewhere between Orange, Texas and Lake Charles, Louisiana, we found some tourist cabins and stopped for the night. It was very late and it had been a long day and we were tired. Rose still had her work to do sterilizing Linda's bottles and making formula, but at last day six was over and we turned in for some rest.

Day 7 and for the second time on the trip I remember breakfast. We were up early as always and decided to eat before we hit the road. It was a typical country café where we ate. For the first time since I had attended machinist's mate school in Norfolk, Virginia in 1940, grits were served with the bacon and eggs. I had never eaten grits in Norfolk because it always reminded me of cream of wheat, which I ate at home during the depression, and never cared for it. This morning I was hungry and decided to try it, and have liked it ever since. Once breakfast was finished, we were on the road again.

We were still following US 90, through New Orleans, which would take us south through the delta before it turned north again to New Orleans. That was out of our way, so just before US 90 turned south we turned north and picked up US 190. We followed US 190 to Slidell, Louisiana where it joined US 90. We were now beginning to get close to the gulf coast and signs of hurricane damage became evident. The autumn of 1947 had been a bad year for storms. Before we started our current journey, there had been several bad hurricanes, which had inflicted heavy damage to the gulf coast area. Key West had some near misses from two or three hurricanes.

It was starting to get dark and the further east we drove the more damage we saw. Beautiful southern homes had been completely demolished; there were rows of homes literally torn apart. Many sections of the concrete highway were washed away, some sections stood upright on their edges as if a bomb had blasted them. It was an eerie feeling as we drove along slowly through this carnage; we seemed to be the only car on the road and our headlights flashing on the concrete sections reflected back to us as we felt our way along. It appeared as if there had been little or no repairs made to the damaged roadway and had many detours. We eventually cleared the area and were happy to leave all the wreckage behind us. We had gained considerable knowledge on the power of a big hurricane. We had been through a couple in Key West but nothing like this.

At last, we reached Pensacola, Florida where we stopped at the first tourist cabins we saw. Tomorrow we planned to take US 98 along the gulf coast and join up with US Alt. 27 at Perry, Florida. We would bypass Tallahassee, which I thought would be a shorter route. Day 7 had been uneventful except, for our encounter with the hurricane damaged area, just another long day's drive. By this time we could follow our routine by rote; our main objective at the end of the day was to get some rest.

It had rained during the night and when we awakened, there was still a light drizzle. We conducted our daily preparations and then stopped at a café for breakfast. I think it was at the café that we found out that US 98 was closed and we would have to take US 90 as a detour. A section of the wooden bridge that crossed Pensacola Bay had sustained damage from a fire; that was why it was closed. We had no other choice so we left Pensacola headed for Tallahassee. In the end, this proved to be a better route than the one I had intended taking. US 98 that ran along the gulf coast would have been several miles longer.

It was a pleasant change of scenery from the desert we had crossed in the west. Northern Florida had an abundance of pine trees and the forest seemed to run on forever. The miles rolled by and we passed through Tallahassee and turned south on US 27, which merged with US 19. We continued on this route until we reached Dunnellon; there we joined US 41 and we would follow this until we arrived at US 27 and then turn due south for Key West. The last leg of our journey would be on US 1. The day was drawing to an end when we passed through Tampa and St. Petersburg; it was time to start thinking of where we would stop for the night. My memory is vague on where we stopped, but I think it was Bradenton. I know we were tired in spite of a pleasant day's drive; eight long days of travel had taken its toll on us. Hopefully tomorrow we would be back to our new home in Key West. Our new quarters at the Navy Seaplane Base should be awaiting us.

It has always been my experience that the closer you get to your final destination the fatigue that has set in from the long trip seems to fade, and you become rejuvenated. When we awoke on our final day, I seemed ready for the road and all the problems we had were far in the past. It was a sunny day and warm as we headed out. In due time we passed the little town of Punta Gorda, where we had spent our first night after leaving Key West. That seemed so long ago, and the fact that we had almost crisscrossed the entire continent on our trip to Idaho and back was hard to comprehend.

At last, we entered Naples, Florida where the highway turned east. Here we started our trek across the Florida peninsula on Alligator Alley. I am not sure that was the official name of this section of highway, but today there is an Alligator Alley and it is the freeway located some miles to the north that runs parallel to the old highway that we were traveling. When we crossed this area, on our way north, it was nighttime and you could only see what was alongside the road. In the daylight, the scenery was entirely different, and for miles on each side of the highway was the Everglades swamp. The alligators were still there, which gave one the feeling of being in Africa. There were few places where one could turn off the highway; we were quite happy to leave that all behind.

At the intersection of US 41 and Florida State 27, we turned due south toward Homestead; here we joined US 1. At last we were on the last leg of our trip; soon we would be on the overseas section of the highway with all of its bridges and the ocean on each side. Rose and I were never fond of duty in Key West, but it would look very good to us after all the many miles we had driven.

We passed Boca Chica Naval Air Station and then on to the housing area of Poinciana, where we had lived prior to our trip. Our neighbor there, Candy Candeleria, had the key to our new apartment at the Naval Seaplane Base; she had moved our few belongings to our new quarters while we were away. Rose and I have commented on the fact that we probably had more of our things with us on the trip than Candy had to move. We did not own much in the early days of our marriage. I have often told her that all I was able to give her when we got married was my love and a steady job, the navy.

Our apartment at the Seaplane Base was number 44; it was on the ground floor and compared to what we had lived in at Poinciana it was a palace. We opened the door and on the floor neatly piled was all we owned. We were home and all the many miles we had traveled were now just memories to recall some day in the distant future. How many miles we drove I can only estimate, but it was somewhere between 8,000 and 9,000 miles; that is not as the crow flies.

Looking back now, after almost 64 years, we wonder what in the world were we thinking when we decided to make this journey. We had a six weeks old baby, it was wintertime to the north and our car, though sound, was 13 years old. It had to be our youth and positive belief in ourselves to make such a decision. Would we do it again, probably, because in spite of the problems we encountered we mastered them and had a ball doing it, and we got to show off our sweet new baby daughter.

The next morning I reported in from my leave. Sometime during the day I was in the head (washroom/toilet) and one of the men who worked for me said, "Where have you been Chief, have you been sick?" I told him, no, I had been on leave. I asked him why he thought I had been sick, his reply was, "you look like hell". I looked in the mirror and thought I do look a little gaunt. I got on the scales in the shop to weigh myself and I had lost fifteen pounds on the trip. Those many long hours on the road had taken their toll. The "trip" indeed had become a journey.

A Friends Impact

The days have slipped by, and suddenly they are molded into years, and you realize that you are alone. The memories you relate to those around you fall on deaf ears; you are of another time, another world to them. The life you lived and the time you spent in your younger years, as in my case in the Navy, are not relative. The sea stories you tell of events long past, developed in an era that is now history, but not understood leaves you cold, for once again no one can relate. Those buddies that you assumed would always be there simply vanished from your world. Suddenly you accept that you are old, as we all become in time.

You do not give up though you keep reaching out trying to grasp the feelings and understanding of those around you. One day you suddenly make contact with one with whom you served some fifty years ago. A stroke of fate cast an old friend into your realm of being. You had been in contact briefly over the past few years, but unlike all old acquaintances that had slipped away, this friend is still there. A Marine reunion, and he was the epitome of the Corps, unexpectedly was scheduled near your hometown, and he came.

Suddenly your life was brightened with this ray of information, and mentally you started planning the meeting. You wondered how you would look to him after all these years. Would there still be the connection of having served together so long ago. A phone call announced his arrival and a meeting scheduled. The drive to his hotel produced another thought, would I recognize him. There were minutes of waiting on our arrival, and then he appeared, older, aged, but fifty years had not changed his looks that much. We greeted each other with a handshake that reached back five decades, but filled with the firmness of friendship formed those long years ago.

I invited him to lunch, which he insisted was on him and after a brief visit at our home we dined. Our time together was only two hours duration, but I was once again with an old friend and we understood the stories each of us told. We brought each other up-to-date on our lives in and out of the service after our last parting. The professional loneliness that I had often felt slipped away as we talked. The years carried on my shoulders, for this short time, fell away and I was deeply moved. The conversation though brief composed a symphony of memories and I was young again. However, his time to leave arrived and we promised to keep in touch. Once again, a firm handshake, as in our initial greeting, sealed our parting. His broad back disappeared through the hotel entrance; I slipped the car into gear and drove away, extremely happy at our meeting but with a tear in my eye at our parting.

For two brief hours, this friend brought a warm glow into my life. I realized the power of friendship and how it can prevail, even after fifty long years of separation. Our common bond of service to our country had brought us together in the beginning and now still sustained us as old men. I will always cherish this brief time together

Last Cruise

This is the story of the last cruise of the USS Wyandot AKA 92 as a commissioned vessel of the United States Navy. The theme of this story revolves around the professional relationship of the Engineering Officer and the Commanding Officer. I have omitted his name, as he has long ago slipped his anchor to his final anchorage.

The Moore Dry Dock Company at Oakland, California built the Wyandot. She was launched on 28 June, 1944, and three months later she was commissioned. She served briefly in the Pacific at the end of WW II, sustaining bomb damage by a Japanese plane. In November of 1945, she was transferred to the Atlantic Fleet, where she served until 1959. During this time, she was outfitted for Arctic and Antarctic operations. Her last cruise was 1958/1959 Deep Freeze four to the Antarctic, and this is that story.

The silence of the ship belied her mission as a working ship; there should have been a clamor of voices, the creaking of machinery, and the gentle rolling of a ship underway. All was unusually quiet. I pushed open the hatch to the outer deck and closed it behind me. The only sound was the noise of the ship's ventilation blowers. There was absolutely no activity topside. I gazed out to the sea, but all that was there was solid ice. However, this is not the beginning of this tale.

It was August of 1958; I was currently assigned as Officer in Charge of the Navy's Shipboard Fire Fighting School at Fleet Training Center, Norfolk, Virginia. My tour of duty there was nearly over and I would soon be assigned to a new duty station. I had received a copy of my relief's orders, but had not received any information as to where I would go. It was common practice, if one chose to do so, to go to Washington, DC to the Bureau of Naval Personnel and check on duty stations that might be available to you. I decided to avail myself of this opportunity.

At home I discussed this with my wife, Rose Ann, and we decided we would take a couple of days leave and drive up to the Bureau, as navy men referred to it, and see what developed as to my next duty station. We arranged for a friend of ours to take care of our daughter while we were away. A couple of days later, after I had been granted my leave, we departed for Washington DC.

We left early in order to enjoy the cooler hours of the day. It was August and our 1954 Oldsmobile did not have air conditioning. The drive up was enjoyable and the Virginia countryside as always was beautiful. This was my first trip to Washington to visit and I was apprehensive about the traffic and the possibility of finding a parking space near the Bureau. We had no problem and after parking the car, I left to see what my future assignment might be. Rose stayed in the car; by this time it was becoming uncomfortable as the day was beginning to get very warm; I hoped I would not be gone long.

I entered the building and in a short time, I located the assignment and detail office for Lieutenants, which was my rank at that time, having recently been promoted. I introduced myself to the civilian lady behind the desk. I told her I was interested in my next duty assignment. Many positions were filled by civilian personnel, so I was not surprised to find her there rather than a sailor. She turned to a file cabinet and promptly produced my service record. I was startled at her expediency in finding my file; it was almost as if she was expecting me. She laid my service record on the desk in front of her and I noticed some sort of marker on the file. She hastily said you were not supposed to see that, but she failed to tell me why it was there. I never found out.

Our conversation started with the duty stations that were available to me. The first one was Main Propulsion Assistant in the USS Providence CL 82, a cruiser, next came Engineering Officer in the USS Fremont APA 44, an amphibious attack transport, and finally Engineering Officer in the USS Wyandot KA 92. She explained to me that Wyandot was assigned to the Atlantic Service Force and was involved with supply missions to the Antarctic. The Wyandot as noted earlier in this narrative was originally commissioned as an AKA, but when transferred from the Amphibious Force to the Service Force she was designated an AK. I may have been a bit vain in my choice, but I preferred to an assignment that I would be a department head rather than an assistant, as would be the case in USS Providence. I declined that offer and we discussed mainly the Wyandot vacancy. She informed me that the Wyandot would be leaving in the fall for the Antarctic as supply ship for Operation Deep Freeze Four. At this point, I only displayed a curiosity of the forthcoming Wyandot operation.

I rather guessed she sensed my interest in the Wyandot, because she called me closer to her desk and pointed to a picture under the glass covering the desk. The picture was of a man with a full red beard; he was clad in full sixteenth century armor and presented a striking pose. She told me that he had played the part of Captain John Smith in the Jamestown Virginia Exposition Pageant. I had to confess he certainly looked the part. At the same time, I was looking at the picture I wondered what kind of a character is this guy. At this point in our conversation, I was still not convinced that any of the three choices was what I wanted, but the chance of a new adventure and experience with the Wyandot billet rather excited me. I think she sensed this, so on my departure I thanked her for her kindness and patience with all the questions I had asked and told her I would leave the decision up to her and her superiors.

I left her office and entered the hallway leading out of the building. The hallway had high ceilings and it was cool inside. The noise of my footsteps seemed to be the loudest noise in the building; the muted sounds from the typewriters and the whirring of the mimeograph machines belied the activity and importance of the operations in this building. All the navy records, assignment and reassignments were conducted here. All personnel activities evolved from this building. The sound of my footsteps slowly faded into the vast immensity of the many hallways; I could see the glaring light from the sun outside as I approached the entrance I regretted leaving the coolness, but I remembered my Rose sitting in that hot car in the parking lot and I hurried on my way. The humid heat of Washington DC hit me in the face as I closed the door to the cool building. The city was built on what a couple of centuries ago was a swamp. The swamp was gone but the heat and humidity, particularly in August, remained. It did not take long for my uniform to show the results of the heat; I began to perspire profusely. Upon reaching the car, I told Rose of my conversation with the lady at the detail desk and the options that were available to me. I gave her a brief account of the Wyandot's forthcoming operations, and told her I bet they were cutting my orders to her at this moment and they would probably be in Norfolk before we got there.

It was past mid-day when I completed my business so we decided to stay a day before going back to Norfolk. I suggested we get a hotel room, and thought we might go to the Willard. I had heard of it, but had no idea that it was where many of the affluent and noted visitors to Washington DC stayed. We drove by and I soon realized that was not the place for us. We decided we would drive to Elkton, Maryland, where we lived when I was stationed at Bainbridge Naval

Training Center, and look around. We did this and on our way back toward Baltimore we spotted a motel and decided to rent a room for the night. It also was very hot and the air conditioning, if they had any, would feel good.

Rose and I had not brought any luggage with us; I think we had toilet articles and that was all. We registered at the motel office and the lady clerk gave us a rather sour look, as if I had just picked up Rose and we were going in for a quickie. We went to our rented cabin and Rose checked the bed and said she could not sleep in that lumpy thing. I tried to talk her into staying, but she said no. I have never been fond of having to return something to a store, and asking for our money back for the room was too much for me. I had to return too many things during the depression, when my stepmother was dissatisfied with something or other. Rose said she would do it, so when she told the lady clerk she wanted our money back because the bed was not suitable to sleep on, the lady came storming over to the cabin expecting to see the bed used. It was not and she reluctantly refunded our money.

We got in the car and drove away laughing because the lady at the motel was obviously unhappy when she looked at our room and things were not as she supposed they would be. We drove as far as Glen Burnie, Maryland and found a decent place to stay. The next day we drove back to our home In Norfolk. The following day I checked in off my short leave and sure enough, my orders for the Wyandot had arrived.

Shortly after our return from Washington, my relief reported aboard for duty. A few days were spent orienting him to the Fire Fighting School operation and its responsibilities. Upon completion of this procedure, he relieved me. My orders granted me some leave before reporting to the Wyandot. I spent this time with my wife, Rose Ann, and daughter, Linda. We knew I would be gone for at least five months; it was a long ways from Norfolk to Antarctica and back, I could not be of any help if they needed me. One evening during this time, my wife and I went to the local shopping mall for a loaf of bread. While at the mall, we looked in the window of a TV store and came home with a new TV, our first one, plus the loaf of bread. This turned out to be good decision for it would give Rose and Linda some entertainment during the months I would be away.

The day for me to report aboard the Wyandot arrived. I had to check the ship's location to find out where she was moored. The Fire Fighting School was located on a section of land that was part of the Naval Supply Depot, and Wyandot was moored outboard of one of the Navy's large repair ships, which was also moored to one of the Supply Depot's piers. I found out after I reported aboard that Wyandot had just finished an overhaul at the Portsmouth, Virginia Navy Yard; she was alongside the repair ship for final shipboard maintenance. This bit of information raised my spirits, for I thought I would have an Engineering Department that will be in top shape for sea. I was very premature in my assumption.

As I crossed the gangway from the repair ship to the Wyandot, I got my first glimpse of my new home. Her lines were very similar to the ones of the first ship I had served on, the USS Tangier AV8, a large seaplane tender. The Tangier had been built at the same shipyard as the Wyandot, but she was a C3 Hull design, whereas the Wyandot was a C2 Hull. Their characteristics were similar, but Wyandot was a slightly smaller ship. The engineering plants I knew would be very similar; the machinery might be of different manufacturers but the plant layout would be almost the same. I could spend more time learning other aspects of the ship that fell under the responsibility of the Engineering Officer. I was happy about that. Every system on the ship except Gunnery, Navigation, Deck, and Communication was the responsibility of the Engineering Officer. That covered many machinery and piping systems. This would be my first assignment as an Engineering Officer, commonly called the Chief Engineer, and I hoped I was ready for the job.

Upon reaching the Quarterdeck of the Wyandot, I faced aft, saluted the colors and then requested permission from the Officer of the Deck to come aboard. This was Navy procedure. I saluted the OD, handed him my orders and introduced myself. I was promptly escorted to the Executive Officer's Quarters and further introduced to him. His name was LCDR (name intentionally omitted). At this point, I was told that the officer I was to relieve had already been detached. I would be informed of the ship's engineering status by the Electrical Officer, who was acting as Engineering Officer. I was not happy about this situation; if there were any important discrepancies on my inspection of all the ship's engineering equipment and systems, then, there was no one responsible that I could confront with the problem. The officer that I was to relieve had been in the same class as I, when we were commissioned at the US Navy Base at Newport, Rhode Island in 1954. I knew a bit of his background and hoped he had run a good department on the Wyandot.

After a short conversation with the Executive Officer, he escorted me to the Captain's cabin. He knocked on his door and we were told to come in. My first glimpse of him came as a surprise, for there he stood with his full red beard just as he had appeared in the picture on the ladies desk back at the Bureau of Naval Personnel. The Captain greeted me and welcomed me aboard, but for some reason I got the feeling, this man is still playing the part of Captain John Smith. I do not recall our conversation from that point on; it was general in nature. The Executive Officer and I excused ourselves, and I was shown to my stateroom and proceeded to move my personal gear aboard. Shortly thereafter, I met my Electrical Officer, who was also the Damage Control Officer, and my Chief Warrant Machinist, who was the Main Propulsion Assistant (MPA).

The next day I commenced making my rounds and inspection of the Engineering Department. This took several days and in the meantime I was keeping notes on which to base my report of findings to the Commanding Officer. My inspection accompanied by the MPA of the main engines and the reduction gears found no problems The Electrical Officer told me of a problem with the electric forced draft blowers for the two boilers. He told me the motors had failed, at times, because of an accumulation of soot, carbon to be exact, in the motor windings due to leaking boiler stack gas. I examined the boilers and found that many of the access covers to the boiler casings were warped. This allowed the stack gas to escape and be drawn into the motor windings, which in time caused the armature to fail. Tightening the access covers did not correct the problem.

There was another item concerning the boilers. The boilers were installed side by side and when I stood on the floor plates in front of the boilers and looked up toward the uptakes, the area over the boilers, I could see a two inch gap at the top between the two boilers. I did not like this at all. I knew the sagging boilers had occurred over time and could not be corrected during a regular overhaul, I could not believe the blower problem had not been corrected during the ship's recent overhaul. I added that to my list of notes. This situation posed the biggest problem in the engine and fire room area.

During the following days, my inspection took me to other parts of the ship. On the main deck forward, there was a compartment by the forward king posts where cargo booms were located. The motors for the booms winches were electric motors and the control panel for the motors was inside the compartment. The hatch doors to the compartment were warped and therefore not completely water tight. Over time, during foul weather, the heavy seas caused salt spray to enter the compartment. This had caused many of the electrical parts to become corroded, under heavy use of the motor driven winches the contacts on the switches would trip and the motors would fail to run. This proved to be a real problem later on, when we had to offload cargo in Antarctica's McMurdo Sound.

I was beginning to have grave doubts about this ship's capabilities to perform the upcoming deployment. My next inspection was the after cargo hold. Once the cargo would be offloaded, this hold would be filled with seawater for added ballast; this had been standard procedure on past cruises to Antarctica. The reason for using this hold for seawater ballast was once all cargo was off the ship it became lighter. Added to this was the fact that the fuel oil supply for the boilers was also at a low level due to consumption since the ship had last refueled. Ballast had to be added to the after part of the ship in order to get the ship's screw propeller below the water line, in order to assure proper maneuverability and efficiency of the screw. Electrical power to this hold had been secured because of its use as a ballast tank, so there was no lighting available. This was an inconvenience but not a problem. The one concern I had was, do the remote controls for the bilge valves work. This was very important when it came time to pump out the seawater that had been used for ballast. If they did not work, there was no way to get into the hold full of water and open the valves by hand. I made a special note of this.

In the meantime, all departments were busy getting ready for our deployment. I finished my report of my inspection and findings of the Engineering Department, with my comments and recommendations, and submitted it to the Captain. He read my report, but did not seem overly concerned with what I had reported. He never indicated to me that he had been previously informed of my findings. He had only recently assumed command of the Wyandot, and I had no idea what the previous Commanding Officer might have relayed to him prior to being relieved of the command. I was beginning to wonder how this forthcoming deployment would play out. There was something about this Captain, which at this time I could not comprehend.

The Wyandot completed her alongside availability with the repair ship and moved to a pier at the US Naval Station. This was my first time underway on a ship in over two years, and it felt good to feel the deck under me again. My time was now being consumed with learning the ship's regulations, reading the current department reports as well as appraising myself of my assigned personnel. I also had to become familiar with the required engineering reports to the Wyandot's type commander, Commander Service Force US Atlantic Fleet. The ship was now engaged in loading part of the cargo that was destined for delivery at McMurdo Sound in Antarctica. The remainder of the cargo would be loaded at Davisville, Rhode Island as well as some Sea Bee Personnel. That meant we would sail north before we headed south to Antarctica. This short deployment would give me a chance to see how the engineering plant and the engineering personnel performed. During this period, I also made an appointment, through the Executive Officer, with the Captain to pay Rose and my courtesy call. This is standard Navy protocol. The call went well and we enjoyed the Captain's and his wife's hospitality.

Time was fast slipping by and my time spent with my family was diminished due to the requirements of learning my new ship and responsibilities. The month of October was nearly over when the ship set sail for Davisville, Rhode Island. One early morning the special sea detail was set and we were on our way. Outward bound we passed Cape Charles to port, changed course to a northerly direction and the Captain rang up Flank Speed. That meant steaming at the maximum speed the ship could make. In the engine room, we increased fires in the boilers and commenced to settle down for a routine steaming watch. I soon found out that this speed was not enough for the Captain and he ordered me to increase it more.

At this point, we were making as much speed as we could and remain within the designed steam pressure and boiler firing rate. I was becoming concerned and voiced my concern to the Captain. I explained that the ship had undergone numerous changes dictated by the demands of her duty in the Arctic and Antarctic, such as the added plating to the hull as well as the ice fins forward of the screw. The alterations I presented to the Captain had reduced the capability of the ship to perform as she had when first commissioned. He did not buy it, so we continued to steam along under what I called forced conditions. At the rate we were firing the boilers I knew the escaping stack gas from the warped cover plates of the boiler casing would increase. I remembered the potential problem with the electric forced draft blowers and this worried me.

We were into the second day at sea when the electric forced draft blower on number two boiler failed. The escaping soot from the leaking cover plates on the boiler had been drawn into the motor, which grounded the armature. There was nothing that could be done but secure the blower. There was no spare armature on board and the ship's engineering personnel did not have the facilities to repair it. I informed the Captain of the casualty and drafted my first

125

Engineering Casualty Report to Commander Service Force, Atlantic Fleet, and to the Bureau of Ships. I also drafted a message, requesting repair to the forced draft blower. These reports and messages were submitted to the Captain, which he released for transmission. I expected to get an approved work request for repairs to our damaged armature, instead the ship was told to submit a request to the Naval Supply Depot at Mechanicsburg, Pennsylvania for a new forced draft blower assembly. The new blower would be airlifted to Davisville, Rhode Island. My engineering personnel would then install it, after removing the damaged one. I knew this would be a challenging operation as our time in port at Davisville was limited.

The Supply Officer and I prepared and submitted the required purchase request for the new blower assembly. The Naval Supply Depot had informed us that they had two blowers in stock, one right hand rotation and one left hand rotation. In our request, we specifically submitted the correct rotation as was installed in Wyandot. In the meantime, my engineering personnel were preparing to remove the damaged blower. This information was relayed to the Captain, who then informed me that the Deck Force would be in charge of removing the blower once we had it unbolted from the boiler ductwork. He said they had more experience with block and tackle than the engineers did; I questioned this in my mind. My experience had shown that engineers frequently move heavy machinery with the use of block and tackle and chain falls. I was sure that my men could do the job, but orders are orders.

The ship continued on its course to Rhode Island at reduced speed. All the doubts that had built up in my mind about the reliability of the boilers and the forced draft blowers once again started to plague me. My first two days at sea in Wyandot had produced my first engineering material casualty, and the deployment to Antarctica had not even started. If the Captain continued to push the Wyandot to her maximum speed for the entire cruise, it would be difficult to analyze the consequences. I soon found that at present this was the least of my problems. On our arrival at Davisville, we found that our replacement blower assembly was waiting for us, but upon examination we found it was of the wrong rotation. The Supply Depot at Mechanicsburg had shipped the wrong one. Now more time would be lost waiting for the right one to be delivered.

I do not know what repercussions might have taken place in Mechanicsburg when it was disclosed that they had sent the wrong blower. The ships supply officer and I knew we had sent the correct information to them when we ordered the new blower; we had paid particular attention to the fact that there was a difference in rotation of the blowers and we made sure we had provided Mechanicsburg with the right data. In the meantime, while we were waiting for the correct blower to arrive, the ships engineers busied themselves with the task of removing the damaged one. Once the blower was disconnected from the ductwork of the boiler the deck force hoisted it clear of its foundation and deposited it on deck. The new blower arrived shortly thereafter, in spite of my doubts that it would get there in time for my men to install it.

In the meantime, the ship's routine went on as usual. The remainder of the cargo that we were to carry to McMurdo Station was loaded and the Sea Bee personnel we were to take with us reported aboard. An all hands personnel inspection was held on the dock. I accompanied the Captain as he inspected the Engineering Department and he found all hands ship shape. This was the first personnel inspection of all hands since I had reported for duty, and I was pleased with my men's appearance.

Our return to Norfolk was fast approaching when the new blower arrived. The around the clock work to install it began. The deck force lowered the blower into place, but no more expeditiously than my men could have done. The most difficult part of the installation was aligning the bolt holes on the blower to the ones in the boiler duct casing. Over time the foundation and boiler had settled, as all ships structures do to a certain degree. This is caused by the various stresses and changes occurring from age, weight distribution, etc. The bolt holes had to be worked into alignment by the use of a pry bar. This took time and a lot of effort, but it was accomplished. The electric motor was connected to the electrical wiring and the forced draft blower was tested. It worked fine and we were back in business with boiler number two, at least for the time being. The leaking boiler casings persisted, only time would tell what the consequences might be.

All repairs now completed we were ready to go to sea again; the month of October was ending and it was time to head south for Norfolk. One of the boilers was scheduled for fireside cleaning in Norfolk, before our departure for the Antarctic, and we would clean the other one in Panama. Regulations required that firesides be cleaned every six hundred hours of steaming, unless operational requirements dictated otherwise. It was obvious that on this deployment the six hundred hour rule would have to be exceeded. Soot and carbon tends to build up on the boiler tubes because of the combustion of fuel oil. Dirty tubes reduce the efficiency of the boilers as well as contributing to possible tube damage and subsequent failure.

The day for departure came and once again, the special sea detail was set. All lines were cast off and we were underway. The air was clear but cool with the feel of the New England autumn. The ship steamed slowly out the channel of Narragansset Bay; the special sea detail was still set and my station was in the engine room, which was main control. I observed that all watch personnel were sharp and attentive to their duties. I was satisfied they knew their jobs well. Shortly thereafter, the special sea detail was secured and the regular watch personnel took over. I informed the watch officer I was leaving and I proceeded to go topside. Block Island was off our beam and we were beginning to change to a southerly course for Norfolk. As usual, flank speed had been rung up on the engine order telegraph; my argument against this was ignored. The ship's crew assumed the usual at sea routine, and I went about my duties.

Considerable thought had been directed to the forced draft blowers and the problem with the leaking stack gas, which had been the cause of the recent blower failure. It was decided that an external source of fresh clean air would be provided by the use of portable electric blowers. These were positioned in the passageway adjacent to the forced draft blowers and flexible ducting was run from them to the forced draft blowers' electric motors. It was hoped that this solution would provide cleaner air and at the same time keep the contaminated air away from the electric motors. Only time would tell if this would work. It was the only workable solution we could devise. It was not feasible to correct the warped boiler inspection plates. The operational commitment of the ship precluded this.

The Wyandot, now fully loaded, surged through the rolling swells of the Atlantic as she plowed along on her southerly course. The creaking of the topside rigging was in cadence with the rolling swells and all seemed well as we steamed along. Approximately eight hours south of Block Island, I was summoned to the engine room, there was a boiler casualty. Number 2 boilers had to be shut down and fires secured. The refractory insulation at the boiler deck rear corbel had failed. Flames were shooting out into the fire room space. I personally informed the Captain of this; it was the second engineering material casualty of this deployment and we had not even started on the main venture of this trip. I prepared and the Captain released the required messages informing all required recipients of our situation. The ship's engineering personnel would have a heavy work load to perform before our scheduled departure. This would include cleaning a boiler and repairing the failed corbel.

Speed was reduced and we steamed along on one boiler operation. The few days passed and at last Cape Henry was sighted and we entered Chesapeake Bay. The ship proceeded to its assigned docking space. It was decided that both boilers would be cleaned inasmuch as boiler number two would be down for repairs. The ship had moored where shore power and steam would be available, so there was no problem in securing the ships boilers. As soon as the boilers cooled, work commenced to clean and repair them. This should have been a relatively routine procedure, but nothing so far with this ships engineering plant was routine.

Once the boilers were cleaned, and this was accomplished with no problems, then a hydrostatic test had to be conducted to determine the water tightness of the boiler tubes and fittings. Both boilers were tested and both had leaking deck tubes. The deck tubes were covered by fire bricks and insulation, which had to be removed to determine which deck tubes were leaking. At this point, the repair crews of two Repair Ships were called in to assist. On their arrival, they immediately started removing the boiler deck insulation. As they worked I stood there and tried to adjust my thinking as to what lie ahead for this ship, and could she make the 25,000 miles journey to the Antarctic and back.

I reported my concern to the Captain and he accompanied me to the Fire Room. I showed him the problems and the difficulties the repair crews were having in getting a satisfactory hydrostatic test of the boilers. They had rolled the tube necks where they passed through the tube sheets, but they still leaked under pressure. I told the Captain that this condition must have existed when the ship was under overhaul at the navy yard. I also told him I was not sure under these conditions if I could assure him of a reliable engineering plant for the upcoming deployment. He responded that maybe an Inspection and Survey Board should be requested to determine the ships sea worthiness. I heartily concurred and that was the last I heard of that. My immediate thoughts were, "he relieved the former Captain under these circumstances, was he afraid of any consequences."

Work continued on both boilers, the repair crews relieving each other and continuing to work to correct the problems. For three days, without sleep, I stood by, observed and checked on progress. This was my problem and I had to see it through to completion. My physical and mental condition was beginning to degrade and the ship's doctor noticed the problem. He informed the Captain and I was given medication and sent home to get some rest. I was completely worn out and slept for over twenty four hours before returning to the ship.

In the meantime, work progressed and the ship was made ready to get underway. A satisfactory hydrostatic test was finally achieved when feed water of a higher temperature was used for the test. The feed water formerly used was too cold and the tubing metal had shrunk to a degree where leakage could occur. This at least was the repair crew's conclusion. I prayed they were right. The boiler fires were lighted and there were no problems. My thoughts were, "there is going to be many hours of steaming at flank speed ahead of us, will all go well."

These repairs had delayed the ships departure by a few days. During this time, I had not been able to spend any real time with Rose or Linda, but duty always comes first. You are not always happy about that. Under such circumstances, I always remembered what some of the old hands used to say, "If the Navy wanted you to have a family they would have issued you one." Departure day arrived, it was 13 November, 1958 and it was Rose's birthday. We said our goodbye and hugged each other; it would be a long time before we could do that again. The special sea detail was set, the lines cast off, four blasts of the ships horn were sounded, indicating my engines are going astern to back clear of the dock, and we were underway for Antarctica and McMurdo Sound.

Once underway all hands settled down to the sometimes monotonous routine at sea. All divisions made sure all their assigned spaces and equipment were properly secured for any rough seas that the ship might encounter. Once again, I asked the Chief in charge of damage control to make sure the remote controls for the bilge valves in the after hold operated properly. He assured me they did. I was spending a good deal of my time learning as much as I could about cold weather procedures. I had enrolled in a Navy correspondence course on cold weather operations, but it was of little help for it did not cover ship operations in the Antarctic. Most of my knowledge was gained talking to personnel who had made the trip before. I assured myself that we had ample flexible steam hoses to de-ice topside equipment that might be subject to icing up from inclement weather.

The first part of the deployment passed quickly. In a matter of a few days found us standing by to enter the Panama Canal. There were several ships ahead of us, so we had to standby until our turn. This would be my first crossing of the canal and I looked forward to the experience. One by one, the ships ahead of us entered the canal and at last, it was our time. The progress through the canal is slow but steady. Each lock you pass through requires flooding, which lifts the ship to the next level; the gates of the lock are then slowly opened and you move on to the next one. The last lift lock found us in a fresh water lake, Gatun Lake, which is fed by the Chagres River. We had to anchor here until the locks going down to the Pacific side were clear of traffic. It was interesting to see all the dredging equipment required to keep the channels clear of silt. The abundant rain of the Canal Zone constantly washes soil into the streams surrounding the canal.

There was no stopping for the crew's liberty; the only stop was for refueling and to take on some fresh stores. This was accomplished at Rodman Naval Station. At last, we exited the last lock; the wide Pacific came into view. Once Panama was behind us the next landfall would be New Zealand, and that was three weeks ahead of us. Slowly the land slipped behind us and the long rolling swells of the Pacific took us into its bosom. That wide expanse of sea that stretched ahead of us had no end. The horizon was always there with nothing but sea to embrace you. Suddenly a chill ran up my spine as I slowly absorbed the immensity of that ocean and the dire consequences that might develop if an engineering problem might occur that was beyond my knowledge and experience to correct. The thought of being dead in the water with no immediate help available was awesome.

Two days out of Panama, 21 November, 1958 Wyandot crossed the equator. Planning for this event had started as soon as the ship left Norfolk. It was always a big event for that was the time old Shellbacks, previous crossers, could get their vengeance on Pollywogs, new comers to the domain of Neptune Rex. I had crossed the equator many times in the past; the first time was in February, 1942, shortly after the start of World War II. I had been invited on this crossing to become a member of the Royal Court, but declined because of ongoing duties. I did volunteer to be the royal Barber, and had a ball giving designer haircuts. Many Pollywogs hated me at the time for what I did to their curly locks. They were very happy after we arrived in New Zealand where all the pretty girls thought their haircuts were cool. Like the old saying, "they made out like bandits." All animosity toward me evaporated.

Since reporting onboard my relationship with the Executive Officer had been limited. After he introduced me to the Captain, our relationship was mainly at mealtime in the wardroom. My communication with the Captain had been direct on all matters; I always kept the Executive Officer informed and he seemed to be satisfied with that arrangement. I had come to the conclusion early on that the XO was somewhat intimidated by the Captain. There never seemed to be a flow of communication through the XO to the Department Heads. Things that I thought the XO should be doing were being done by the Captain. One of these was the daily instruction, while underway, by the Captain on general ship procedures etc. for our passage through the ice, once we encountered it. At no time did I find the Captain acknowledging the fact that he had some well qualified young officers onboard who had gained some experience by their previous tours to Antarctica. I continued to feel the Captain was playing a role as if he were performing on stage before a grand audience. I kept seeing in my mind that picture of him on the detailer's desk back at the Bureau of Naval Personnel as Captain John Smith. This man was seeking his role in history.

After the Shellback Initiations were over, the ship settled down for the long voyage that still lay ahead of us. New Zealand was still over two weeks of steaming ahead of us. The monotony of the heat of the tropics and the daily routine quieted down the crew after the celebration of the initiations. In the evening there were movies shown to the crew and the officers. The ship had taken enough movies onboard before our departure to provide entertainment for the cruise. On some evenings the Captain would invite one or two of his junior officers to his quarters for dinner. I had been afforded this invitation on a couple of times. The Captain frequently served curry for the meal, and many of the younger officers were not familiar with this dish or its many condiments. He seemed to relish delight when they were not sure how to apply the condiments to the main dish of curry. I always sensed a condescending attitude on the Captain's part, or perhaps I still had not fully analyzed his character and demeanor.

Thanksgiving Day at sea arrived on November 27 and a grand feast of roast turkey and all the trimmings was served. Cigars and cigarettes were passed out to the crew, which was the custom at the time. We were in the tropics and the heat did not add to the occasion, but all hands had a good time. This was the second event that I had missed with my family so far on this cruise; the first was Rose's birthday, the day we set sail, and now Thanksgiving. There would be other dates of significance in coming days.

Daily instructions by the Captain continued; we were continually drummed by his many incantations of the various ice formations we were to encounter. I wished he had directed as much attention to the operation of the ship's propulsion plant. I was still worried about pushing the old bucket to her maximum speed day after day. So far, our jury rigged portable blowers had kept the forced draft blowers for the boilers working. The soot and stack gas leakage from the boilers continued, but we seemed to have its affects under control. The sea miles rolled astern and vanished in the frothy wake of the calm Pacific. Our route was taking us clear of the usual sea lanes, we had sighted no ships and not an island had we passed that we could view.

The days turned to weeks and finally on 10 December we made landfall. Shortly thereafter, we arrived at port Lyttelton, New Zealand. It had been almost a month since we sailed from Norfolk. Three of those weeks had been spent traversing the Pacific from Panama, our last landfall. New Zealand looked great. Port Lyttelton was the seaport for Christ Church, which lay a few miles to the north over the mountains that bordered the port. Wyandot was assigned a mooring to the docks, and once again it was good to be in port safe and sound.

Once the ship was properly moored liberty call was sounded and all hands, except the duty section, were allowed ashore.

I had little time in Port Lyttelton for shore leave. All the last preparations were being conducted prior to our departure for Antarctica and McMurdo Sound. The ship was refueled, last minute cargo was loaded, mail for the wintering over party was loaded and some distinguished passengers came on board. One of the passengers was Rear Admiral David M. Tyree, who was to relieve Rear Admiral George J Dufek, Commander Task force 43; the other was Sir Raymond Priestly, a veteran Antarctic Explorer. Admiral Tyree, while on board conducted a personnel inspection of the ship's crew. He seemed satisfied with the crew's appearance. I had busied myself with assuring to the best of my ability that the engineering department was prepared and ready for our trip through the ice to McMurdo Station.

The presence on board of Sir Raymond Priestley was quite an honor. Sir Raymond was a geologist and had participated in Antarctic explorations with English explorers Scott and Shackleton in the early 1900's, when such ventures were far more arduous and dangerous than our simple supply mission would be. On several occasions, I had the privilege of talking with him, needless to say, I was in awe of his history. I never had the courage to delve into his experiences, my conversation remained with questions that were current to our mission. Sir Raymond was the epitome of an English gentleman, congenial, reserved, and obviously well educated. I later found that he had held numerous positions in the British government after his polar experiences. His presence on board, by his very prominence, tended to subdue our Captain's striving for adventure notoriety, or so I surmised. By this time, I had developed the thought that our Captain was trying to establish a reputation by which he would be remembered.

The five days we were in port passed quickly and on 15 December the ship set the Special Sea Detail, we cast off all lines and we were underway. The real challenge of the cruise now lie ahead;

foul weather, solid ice flows, proper engineering performance, these possibilities were thoughts in my mind. This would be a completely new experience for me and the problems we had with the boilers were constantly in the back of my mind. The possibility of foul weather worried me, for in the lower latitudes, strong winds and heavy seas could be encountered, and the loss of boiler power or even partial loss could be disastrous. The Captain's continuing desire to push the ship to the maximum speed, despite my respectable words of caution, exacerbated my fears. These apprehensions would be foremost in my mind for many days to come.

It was summertime in New Zealand, cool but pleasant, when we set sail for the Antarctic. On departure from Port Lyttelton Task Group 43.1 was formed, consisting of USS Wyandot KA 92, USS Nespelen AOG 55, and USCGC Northwind, the ice breaker. The Task Group Commander was Captain E. A. McDonald, who flew his flag in Northwind.

Each day we sailed further south the cooler the temperature became. The seas had been relatively calm, but the anxiety of what lie ahead continued to be of concern to me. A few days out of Port Lyttelton, we began to encounter signs of the Antarctic environment as bits of ice appeared in the frigid waters. The temperature indicated on the engine room sea water thermometers was 23 degrees Fahrenheit. Watch personnel in the engine room had to throttle the discharge valves on lube oil coolers in order to maintain a high enough temperature so the oil would not be sub cooled. The same was required of the main engine condensers in order to maintain a proper heat balance of the condensate used for boiler feed water. I was learning a completely new set of engineering procedures.

Slowly but steadily the ice began to become thicker; there was brash ice, then bits of flow ice, bergie bits and on the fifth day we entered the pack ice. The ice breaker, Northwind was slowly breaking a path through the ice for us. Progress at times was very slow, the breaker always looking for a polynia (open water in the ice pack), which would further our advance through the ice. From my observation, the ice appeared to be four to five feet thick, and there were pressure ridges formed as the ice pushed against itself. The only noise was the slow grinding of the ice along the hull of the ship. Sometime during this part of the passage, the Northwind departed to assist the USS Nespelen AOG 55, the smaller ship in the Task Group. Wyandot would continue to try to penetrate the ice on her own.

The ice pack slowly closed in around the ship and it was at this time that the Captain decided to ram his way through. Ice Breakers are designed to ride up on the ice flow and break it by the sheer weight of the ship The Wyandot had been reinforced with steel plating at her waterline to just above her keel and from her bow aft to about frame 147, but she did not have the curved bow that ice breakers have. This added protection was for traversing the loose ice, but the Captain decided to use it for a buffer to ram the ice. The first attempt stopped the ship abruptly and at that time, I hurriedly went below to the engine room. On reaching the engine room I heard the signal from the bridge, "All engines ahead", the exact number of RPM's I do not remember, but at that time I positioned myself on the main engine reduction gears. Stationed there I could tell when and if we encountered ice in the ships screw. The forward motion of the ship was again stopped by the ice pack, and then the order from the bridge was, "All engines astern". Almost immediately, there was a loud noise and the reduction gear housing vibrated heavily; the vibration was of such magnitude that it literally tossed me off my feet. I immediately ordered the engine stopped, and had the engineering officer of the watch notify the bridge that the engine had been stopped. The bridge asked who had ordered such action and they were informed it was the Chief Engineer who ordered the engine stopped. I was promptly ordered to the bridge and to report to the Captain.

On my way to the bridge the thoughts that were going through my mind were what damage had the ship sustained, from backing down into the ice and also what might have happened when the ship rammed the ice trying to break through. The Captain was waiting for me when I arrived on the bridge and his first words were "Why did you stop my engine". I told him," Captain, the ship was chopping ice

137

when it backed down". He asked me how I knew that and I told him because of the vibration in the reduction gears, the loud noise and the fact that it had almost thrown me off the reduction gear housing. He berated me in front of the bridge watch and repeatedly shouted, "Do not ever stop my engines again". I replied, "Aye, Aye Sir" and requested permission to leave the bridge. I do not know if I made my point but he never rammed the ice again nor did he ever back down into the ice again.

Once back in the engine room I had the Officer of the watch make an entry in the Engineering Log to the extent of what happened. My analysis was when the ship backed down it drew large chunks of ice into the screw and because of the ice fins, that had been installed forward of the screw, the ice could not escape the screw. The ice had jammed between the blades of the screw, the hull, and the ice fins. I made an inspection of the reduction gear housing and all of the shaft main bearings as well as carefully listening to the gears the next time the ship moved ahead. I could find no indication of damage and this was entered in the log. I ordered an inspection of the hull plating in the forward part of the ship to determine if there had been any damage sustained when the ship rammed the ice. This inspection disclosed that there was a crack in the hull on the starboard side in the forward ammunition handling room for the forward starboard guns. The crack was approximately five inches in length. This was also reported to the bridge and another entry made in the Engineering Log. I ordered the damage control watch to check each time he made his rounds. Repairs would have to be made once we got moored and the cargo off-loaded. This would allow the crack to rise above the waterline and a welder could make the repair. My real fears were what damage had our screw sustained. There was no way to inspect the crack until after we arrived at McMurdo. Once the ship tied up to the ice shelf, and the cargo unloaded, then the ship would ride high enough in the water and I could see the screw. I hoped it had escaped any damage, but I was extremely doubtful. Its encounter with the blocks of ice, when the Captain had backed the engines, had caused a tremendous jolt to the screw, the shaft and bearings.

It had been a busy day and some of the fears I had, became reality. Any further attempts to break the ice had ceased; the ship settled down to wait for the ice to break up or the return of the ice breaker to break us free. The ship's crew settled down to wait. I reviewed the events of the day with my Main Propulsion Assistant, Chief Warrant Officer Douglas; he was not happy with the way his main engines had been abused and I had to concur. It became a waiting game with only the below decks activity being performed. I occupied my time with catching up on paper work. I frequently checked with the roving damage control watch to ascertain that the crack in the forward hull had not enlarged. I finally turned in for the night, but it really was not night, for we had entered the latitude of perpetual daylight. One had to rely on their watch and calendar to determine night from day. Under these conditions a person could easily over extend himself by not knowing when the regular day had ended.

The next morning I arose to a quiet ship. I had my breakfast, chatted a bit with other officers in the ward room and made my rounds of the below deck engineering spaces. It was ominously quiet, but in the engine room the pressure of the pack ice against the ship's hull was apparent. Standing there on the floor plate's one could hear the creaking of the hull plates, and occasionally some paint would pop off the bulkhead from the intense pressure being exerted on the hull. To see and hear this was unnerving to say the least, and I wondered just how much pressure it takes to crack the ship's hull. It was summer time and the ice flow should be breaking up and moving out to the open sea. It was obvious at this moment that was not happening. How long would the ship and its crew and passengers have to wait before the ice moved or the ice breaker arrived? I decided to go topside and have a look at our surroundings.

The silence of the ship belied her mission as a working ship, there should have been a clamor of voices, the creaking of machinery, and the gentle rolling of a ship underway. All was unusually eerily quiet. I pushed open the hatch to the outer deck and closed it behind me. The only sound was the noise of the ship's ventilation blowers. There was absolutely no topside activity. I gazed out to the sea, but all that was there was solid ice. I looked out across the ice and there at some distance a lone Emperor Penguin was standing, silently, magnificently observing the ship. I assumed he was probably musing on our situation and silently saying to himself, "You got yourself in this situation now how in the hell are you going to get out". He was the only living thing observed as far as the eye could see. Further off our port beam one could see the Antarctic land mass rising to the sky with its huge Ross Ice Shelf. For one brief moment I felt I knew how the early explorers must have felt when they encountered these conditions, but they were in sailing vessels. The steel hull beneath me gave me a greater measure of security even though it was emitting its own creaking of distress.

The days passed slowly and from time to time the ice would part enough to allow the ship some forward progress; then it would close in and hold it in its icy grip once more. The lone Emperor Penguin had disappeared somewhere astern in his icy realm, but one day I observed a solitary Leopard Seal take his place on the ice. It was close enough to the ship so I could see its eyes watch the ship as it moved slowly by. Once again it was the only living thing I could see on that endless stretch of ice. During this period a huge portion of the Ross Ice Shelf had broken off and fallen into the sea. I guessed its length to be several miles. It lay there in the sea motionless, like some icy prehistoric monster waiting to pounce on some unsuspecting victim. I was glad it was at a distance and on a bearing that would not interfere with the ships progress.

Wyandot had entered the ice on 21 December, Rose's and my twelfth wedding anniversary, on 18 December, my birthday, I turned thirty -seven, and on 25 December, Christmas Day we were again locked solid in the ice. Three more family days together had been missed. Many times on the cruise I had thought of my loved ones back in Norfolk, and how much I missed them. This day, Christmas, was very lonely, but there had been other days that we had been apart and we managed to overcome our loneliness. A fine Christmas dinner of ham and again all the trimmings helped make it a day to remember. We all managed to ferret out some Christmas joy and the Captain was discrete enough not to interfere. A good time was had by all. At this time it was discovered that some of the beer supply we had on board for the upcoming wintering over party at McMordo Station was missing. Its whereabouts was never found, but its existence became known when the anchor was dropped on the ice in an attempt to break us free; a shower of empty beer cans poured out of the hawse pipe onto the ice. The culprits had hid their empties there.

Five more days would pass with the Wyandot held fast in the grip of the Antarctic ice. The noise created by the stress of the ice on the hull continued, but at last on 31 December we broke free and entered McMurdo Sound and headed through the open passage created by the ice breaker. We could now proceed to our mooring alongside the pack ice. During this time the ice breaker USS Staten Island GB 5 joined us. The mooring site was several miles out on the ice pack in McMurdo Sound. The ice breaker had broken a relatively smooth edge along the ice for the ship to moor, but there were numerous large chunks that had to be moved. This maneuver would create a situation, which had lasting consequences.

The Wyandot made her approach to the mooring area and passed some of her mooring lines to the line handlers, who had been ordered to help the ship dock. Permanent mooring would follow when holes in the ice had been made and dead men installed to which the mooring lines would be attached. The dead men were put in the holes, the holes filled with water, which froze thus creating a solid cleat to hold the mooring lines. It was at this time that the lose chunks of floating ice came into play. The officer of the deck wanted to maneuver the ship slightly away from the mooring area and work the ice clear with the ships propeller wash. The Captain disagreed and told them to melt the ice with fire hoses, and thereafter he left the bridge to get some sleep. The temperature of the water was about 25 degrees; you do not melt ice at that temperature.

I was not aware of what happened after the Captain left the bridge until the ship completed her mooring. The Commodore, who had left his flagship, the icebreaker, came back to the mooring area and observed the men trying to melt the ice with the fire hoses. He apparently suggested, use the engines to move the ship's stern out from the ice. The chunks of ice could then be pushed clear, with the use of boat hooks. This was done by the bridge watch telling the engine room over the telephone the number of turns to make on the ship's screw; by this method there was no noise made by use of the engine telegraph, which would have alerted the Captain about what was taking place. While this was being done, the Commodore was assisting the men with the boat hooks to move the chunks of ice. The maneuver worked perfectly and Wyandot was drawn up against the ice and properly moored. This action was completed so quietly that I was not even aware the engines were being used; I had left the engine room and was in the Log Room, engineer's office and did not hear any engine noise. How the Captain eventually found out what had taken place I do not know, but he placed all officers concerned on report, including me, and held up submission of their fitness reports for weeks thereafter. The Bureau of Naval Personnel, so I was told, had to issue a direct order to him to get the reports submitted. It was only after he found out the Commodore's involvement that he complied.

Once the Wyandot was moored, preparations began to offload her cargo. Caterpillar tractors with large sleds arrived from McMurdo base, these were parked a short distance from the ship. A survey was made of the ice conditions adjacent to the mooring area. Flags were positioned where cracks were visible, and measurements were taken of the length of the cracks. The ship established a continuous watch on these cracks for the entire time Wyandot was moored to the ice. This was extremely important as any change or enlargement of the cracks could affect the off-loading of the cargo. It was summer time and the ice in the sound could suddenly start to break up and move out to sea. If this happened without prior notice, men, equipment and cargo could be lost. The length of each watch was two hours. At the end of the watch, each man was given two ounces of brandy to warm him. With that reward, you did not mind standing on the cold ice for two hours.

New Year's Day, 1959 found the ship hard at work preparing to unload her cargo. With the advent of summer, it was important that the crew take full advantage of the present stable ice conditions. The off-loading continued around the clock; the large sleds and their tractors maintained a steady train of cargo from the ship to the shore base at McMurdo Station. At about this time the Captain departed on a mountain climbing expedition to Mt. Erebus, located across the sound in Victoria Land. Mt Erebus is the southernmost active volcano on planet earth; it rises to the altitude of 12,448 feet. Why he left the ship at the crucial time in its mission of replenishment can only be left to the speculation that his desire was to establish himself as an explorer. This act would come to the attention of the Admiral in charge of the mission later on. The Captain took one man with him, a seaman who was part of the Sea Bee detachment we had on board, at least that was the information I was given. A helicopter flew them and their meager equipment to the mountain, at what elevation they were dropped off, I do not know. Another bit of my analysis of the Captain started to fall into place.

The offloading of our cargo continued at a brisk pace. There were several occasions during the offloading when the electric winches stopped; this was due to the auxiliary switches in the control panel tripping. I was afraid this would happen when I made my initial inspection of the ship's machinery when I first reported aboard. I had found the electrical panel corroded from seawater leaking in from an ill-fitting watertight door. The engineering department did not have a Chief Electrician at the time. I insisted one be assigned and my wish had been granted. Chief Crisp did a fine job of keeping the winches running.

My time was devoted between my usual duties and standing my assigned ice watch. We had been issued cold weather gear for our watches on the ice, and the insulated boots were appreciated very much. The air temperature was not really cold, as it was summertime, but it was below zero even with the continuous sunshine at this time of the year in Antarctica. The ship was slowly beginning to ride higher in the water as the cargo was offloaded, and I was waiting for the time when I could gain access to the ships screw and see what damage it had sustained from its encounter with the ice.

Our presence on the ice was not without some local inhabitants. There was an abundance of Adelie Penguins in our area. They are the little flightless birds that stand about 28 inches tall, and as we said, always dressed in their formal tuxedoes. That is what their black and white configuration of feathers resembled. They were not frightened of us just wary. Wherever we happened to walk, they seemed to be there or followed us. They were very curious little guys. They scrutinized everything they saw. If something lay on the ice, they would check it over. We called them pipeline inspectors and they were fine company. It was interesting to watch them when they lined up to go into the water for food. They would wait until one of them jumped in and if he were not eaten then the others would join him. We had been instructed not to get close to the water's edge as there were Orca Whales in the area, they were killers, and penguins were there favorite food. This may have been a tall tale as we never saw any evidence of their presence, but the penguins may have had better information than we did.

On two different occasions, I was able to go to McMurdo Station and look over the operation. The base resembled a large construction site. There was heavy equipment everywhere and the muddy volcanic soil formed a continuous mess, duckboards were present at the entrances of all the Quonset huts; these were the structures for most of the buildings. There was a MARS (Military Affiliate Radio Station) where you could call home if and when the atmospheric conditions were right for radio transmission. Your call would be answered by some ham radio operator in the States and he would then patch you in to your home by telephone. I was able to talk to Rose on my second visit by a telephone patch through Toledo, Ohio. She was surprised to say the least when the operator got her out of bed with my call. For a few brief minutes, we were together again.

One of the highlights of a visit to the base was a ride in a Weasel, a tracked vehicle about the size of a large jeep. I had never driven one before, but with a little testing, I got the hang of it. You steered the Weasel by a lever on each side, one pull made you go one way and a pull on the other side made you go that way. My electrical officer went with me and he wanted to drive as he had done it once before, but I pulled rank and did the driving going in. On the way back, I let him drive, just like a couple of kids having fun. It did break the monotony of life aboard ship for a very brief time.

Most of the ship's cargo had been offloaded when the Captain finally returned from his venture to Mt. Erebus. He looked gaunt and was severely sun burned and probably wind burned as well. The off-loading had progressed so smoothly while he was absent; there was only one loss of a piece of cargo. That was a piece of steel plate that had broken loose from the cargo boom and had dropped into the water of McMurdo Sound. This piece was part of a fuel tank for McMurdo Base, which was being assembled by welding personnel of the Sea Bee detachment we had brought with us from Davisville. The ship was able to supply a piece of plate from stores on board. I personally think the Captain's absence contributed to the very smooth operation while he was away. When he was around, he had an affinity for wanting to change things.

By this time, the ship had raised sufficiently in the water so repair to the crack in the hull in the forward section of the ship could be completed. I chose my best welder and he repaired the crack by welding it and also welding a metal plate over that. The ship's screw was now exposed enough for me to make my inspection for any damage that might have occurred with our encounter with the ice chunks. I had the engine room watch engage the main engine jacking gear and start turning the shaft so I could observe each blade of the screw as it broke water. Slowly the blades came into view and two of them moved by with no apparent damage. As the third one appeared, I could see it was bent out-of-line. When the blade was upright, I had the jacking gear stopped. A piece of staging was rigged from the ice to the screw, and with my tape measure, I crawled out to take a measurement of the bent blade. I found that the blade was bent fifteen inches out of true. I looked for any sign of cracks, but could not see any. There could be invisible damage but only a magna-flux test of the metal would disclose this. That would have to be done by a repair facility. My fear of damage had proven valid, now I had to draft a message reporting this to the proper commands.

I returned to the log room and prepared my message to our Service Squadron Commander, Commander Service Force Atlantic Fleet, and the Bureau of Ships. I reported my findings to the Executive Officer and then to the Captain and gave him my draft of the message reporting the damage to the screw. He refused to release the message, this was direct noncompliance with regulations, and I was left speechless. All of this was entered in the Engineering Log, which he later made me alter. I had never, in almost nineteen years of navy experience, been subjected to such disregard for Navy Regulations. I did not appreciate the position in which this placed me. I knew beyond any doubt that once we were underway there would be increased vibrations to the main engine and the main propeller shaft caused by the bent blade, what collateral damage this might cause I could only guess.

The off-loading of the cargo was finally completed and it was now time to commence preparations for our departure. As in prior years the after cargo hold was flooded with sea water in order to increase the draft aft so the screw would be as far below the waterline as possible. This was necessary to give the screw maximum efficiency and protect it from the ice, but it also created a problem. Once the after hold was flooded, it created a draft aft of fifteen feet lower than the draft forward; this made it difficult to maintain an accurate water level in the boilers. Too high a water level in the boilers would cause moisture carry over with the steam to the main steam turbines, which could cause damage to the turbine blades. My hope was that we could clear the ice and rough weather, if we should encounter any, in a short period of time. Then I could pump out the after hold and get the ship back on an even keel. My mind was constantly battling with that nagging problem of the bent screw blade and its possible consequences.

The crew had done a fine job off-loading the cargo and in appreciation the Captain had a ration of beer issued and a party was held on the ice for all hands. Consumption of alcohol on board navy ships, except for medicinal purposes, was not allowed, that is why the party was held on the ice. Everyone had a good time including the penguins, some of the crew gave them beer and they liked it. After their first taste, they were reluctant to leave. A Leopard Seal even made an appearance, but no one tried to give it a ration of grog. It just lay on the ice and watched the party.

There was one bit of historical cargo that was loaded prior to the ship's departure. The airplane that Rear Admiral Byrd had flown and landed at the South Pole was loaded and secured atop the after cargo hold. The plane was a Navy R4D, in commercial use it was a DC3 built by Douglas Aircraft Manufacturer. The name of the plane was Que Sera Sera and was destined for the Naval Aviation Museum. This was the first plane to land at the South Pole. Special care was taken to assure this important piece of cargo was properly secured for the return trip home.

There was one incident that happened, just prior to our departure, which affected me quite deeply. A young Lieutenant Junior Grade came on board; He asked to see the Chief Engineer, which was I. He stated he would be going back with the ship as a passenger and asked if he could stand some watches in the engine room. He was a pilot who had flown missions for the wintering over party, but he also had been an engineer in the Merchant Service. He wanted to refresh himself and improve his experience in the engine room. We had a nice conversation and I told him I would be happy to have him as a student watch stander. He had completed his last flight he said and would move his gear aboard. For some reason at the last minute, he was asked to make one more flight before we were to leave. His plane crashed on that flight and he was killed. They brought his body onboard for our return trip. This incident bothered me for a long time.

On 9 January, 1959, the special sea detail was set and the ship got underway for Port Lyttelton, New Zealand. The outbound passage from McMurdo Sound was slow, but not overly hampered by the ice. The huge mass of ice that had broken free of the Ross ice Shelf still lay huge and menacing on our starboard beam, but at a distance that did not cause the ship any problems or concern. Its length still measured several miles and from all appearances, it would be that size for some time. The Wyandot with its fifteen foot drag must have looked like a twelve foot rowboat with a fifteen horsepower motor at its stern, as it wallowed through the ice. I was anxious to clear the ice and start pumping out the seawater ballast we had in the after hold. The idea of being in the open sea with all that water with the free surface effect did not appeal to me. There were no baffles in the after hold to. It is free surface effect. In a quiet sea, this would be minimal, but a rough sea would certainly exacerbate the situation. Tons of free surging water can affect a ships righting moment, which also affects its handling qualities. This situation added to the bent screw blade continued to gnaw at my innards.

After what seemed endless hours, the ship entered the open sea and the ice gradually fell astern. I issued the order to commence pumping out the after hold. I was told a short time later the remote controls for the bilge valves in the hold could not be opened. No amount of effort with pipe wrenches could move them. I called the chief petty officer, who had told me on several occasions before we left Norfolk that they were operable, and asked him for an answer. He had none. At this point, I was seriously considering taking disciplinary action against the Chief, but doubted the Captain would back me up on this issue. I asked him for any suggestions on how to get the water pumped out; his response was to use the P500 portable gas powered emergency pumps. I told him fine, get them going; they did not work either. The P500 pumps are to be tested regularly, using seawater, and then are to be flushed with fresh water so they will not corrode between testing periods. The P500 pump casing was constructed of aluminum, which corroded very easily when exposed to salt water. This had not been done and so the pumps were useless until they could be dismantled and the corrosion removed. We did not have time for this; that water had to be pumped out one way or another. This was just another surprise along with the boiler forced draft blowers, the leaking boiler tubes, the bent screw, and all ahead flank speed Captain.

After informing the Captain of our problem I retreated to my office, the log room, and commenced going over all the blueprints of the bilge piping system hoping to find some sort of bypass of the after hold bilge valves. There was none and I was not really expecting to find any. While I was pondering all of this, a light bulb came on. I called the chief, who had given me his word that the remote controls on the valves worked, and told him to get me two eductors. We would rig them in the after hold and use the fire pumps to provide the salt water pressure we needed to activate them. The eductor is a device that can be hooked to a two and a half inch fire hose and when lowered into a space that contains water can pump it out. This is performed by creating suction, in the eductor, by passing a stream of water under pressure through an orifice within the eductor. The water pressure is provided by the ship's fire pumps. The efficiency of the eductor is fifty percent; one hundred gallons through the eductor will remove fifty gallons of water. This would be a long drawn out process. It was the only alternative we had to solve our problem. This procedure I remembered from my tour of duty as Officer in Charge of the Navy's Shipboard Firefighting School prior to reporting aboard the Wyandot.

I opened the watertight hatch to the after cargo hold and peered down into the black abyss; it was a turbulent void. The black water was rolling violently from port to starboard, following the ship's movement as it plunging through the rough sea. The only access to the hold was the vertical steel ladder mounted on the forward bulkhead. The only possible place to secure the eductor was to the ladder; that would be challenging piece of work. Each time the ship rolled a huge wave of water would surge up the ladder almost to the hatch opening. I decided that I would attempt to secure the eductor to the ladder at a depth that would provide adequate coverage to the eductor. It was important to maintain it at a depth where it would take suction on the water. I could not send one of my men down there without trying it out myself. We could only use one eductor at a time;

I could only use one fire pump for dewatering. The other pump was held in reserve for firefighting purposes if needed.

I tied a section of line around my chest as a safety line and started my decent into that icy cold water. The eductor was lowered with me by my men tending the securing line. The water surged up and enveloped me to my waist; the bitter cold left me gasping for breath. I could only descend a few rungs on the ladder because of the cold water and the force of its surging. It took all I had to hang on to the ladder. I passed the bitter end of the securing line under the lowest rung I could reach, and passed it up to the men above. This was not the most efficient setup, but under the circumstances, it was the best we could do. The eductor had to be tightly secured otherwise it would thrash around with each surge of the water and would not take a suction. At last, we were ready to cut in the water from the ship's fire pump and start dewatering the hold. I had an extra watch set to monitor the pumping, and then shivering from head to toe I went to my quarters and donned a dry uniform. I then proceeded to the bridge and informed the Captain of our progress.

Once we were clear of the ice, the Captain increased speed and it was then I began to notice the vibration caused by the bent screw. The vibrations were not too severe as long as the speed was moderate, but I was sure they would increase once the after hold was empty of water and the ship resumed its normal fore and aft trim. The Captain was sure to increase our speed to flank speed, which was his method of operation. I became very apprehensive about our future voyage home. Would any severe problems develop?

The dewatering of the after hold continued to be a very slow process. The water level was dropping, but at a very slow rate. Occasionally the eductor had to be lowered in order to keep it submerged for proper suction. I left this to the Chief and his men now that the procedure had been established. Correcting the trim of the ship was taking a long time and the fifteen foot drag was causing some problems with the boiler feed water. The water level in the boilers, as previously mentioned, was difficult to maintain so there would be no feed water carryover with the steam to the engines and auxiliary machinery. There is always a certain amount of steam leakage around valve stems and pump shaft packing glands. Where this occurred, icicles were being formed by the boiler compound in the feed water that was being carried over in spite of the attempt by boiler personnel to control it. Stalactites were visible at almost every valve in the piping system. It gave the engineering spaces an eerie look, like being in a huge cave. Note: Boiler compound is added to boiler feed water to control scale buildup inside of boiler tubes.

Wyandot's crossing from McMurdo Sound to New Zealand was blessed by fair winds and a moderately heavy sea. On 16 January, 1959 one week after departing Antarctica, she arrived at Port Lyttelton. The pumping of the after hold continued the entire crossing. It was only completed after arriving in port. After many hours of use the eductors were relieved of their duty and the main bilge pumps were put to work; this was made possible when the water level dropped to a depth where the after hold bilge valves could be opened by hand. A man wearing hip boots was allowed to descend the ladder into the hold, disconnect the inoperable remote control cables and open the valves. It had been a very long week for me; I had agonized over all the free water sloshing around in the hold and prayed the eductors would do their job. It had been a far from satisfactory solution, but it worked. There had been numerous queries from the Captain, during this time, as to the progress of the pumping, and I had been able to provide satisfactory answers. I continued to be plagued by the circumstances that caused the situation in the first place. I wondered if I had been negligent at the beginning of the cruise even with all the other problems at that time.

Port Lyttelton was a quiet, quaint seaport that languished in an atmosphere, at least to me, of decades past. This feeling continued even more when I got my first visit to Christ Church, a town over the mountain from Port Lyttelton. The people were so friendly and warm hearted; life flowed at a pace reminiscent of my childhood during the 1930's. The city was a beautiful, small one, with flowers and quaint buildings. The Victoria Garden was graced with hundreds of different kinds of Roses, we had just missed their full blooming, but they were still beautiful. The town center had a raised portion of ground with a clock in the center and garnished with all kinds of flowers and plants. It was a beauty to behold. The life style of the city was relaxed with little traffic; one could spend a lifetime here and let the rest of the world roll by.

There was one interesting feature that I had never witnessed before. The pubs closed at 1800 (6:00 PM), after that time you could only purchase beer at a hotel where you had to be registered as a guest. The New Zealand workman was an accomplished consumer of the beverage, and each evening after getting off of work he would stop by the local pub and have a few, and then have a couple of large bottles filled which he could take home. The business was brisk at this time of the day and many customers had to be served in a short period of time. The bartender would serve his client by the use of a long hose with a spigot on the end, in this fashion he could move from one end of the bar to the other and not have to be bothered with opening a bottle or running from drinker to a fixed tap and back. The long hose was attached to a huge barrel or cask hidden somewhere within the confines of the pub. It was a most efficient means of dispersing the local nectar. There were many glasses of Fosters that passed the lips of the thirsty drinkers.

One day the Captain summoned me to his cabin and invited me to accompany him ashore that evening. I was not enthused about this invitation, but you do not deny the Captain's request. At the appointed hour, I met him on the Quarterdeck and we ventured forth on our outing for the evening. The Captain either rented an automobile or granted the use of one, and he was going to be the driver. I had heard rumors of his driving skills. I was not too enthralled about being his passenger. Our departure down the dock was at full throttle and the numerous dock capstans (winches) used to assist ships when docking became goal posts to miss. I thought if he keeps this up this is going to be an interesting evening. Once we cleared the dock, he did settle down. I began to breathe a bit easier. The evening was uneventful; we had a few beers and dinner and then returned to the ship. Our conversation was just idle chatter and no mention was made of the engineering difficulties that had occurred. I had hoped he might show some concern for the bent screw blade, but he seemed oblivious of that. I continued to get the feeling that all the problems we had, happened to someone else and not on his watch as the saying goes.

On one of my visits to Christ Church, I was able to place a long distance overseas telephone call to Rose. There was a wireless and telephone office there and for $9.00, I was able to talk for three minutes. It was so good to hear her voice again and to let her know all was well with me. There was neither time nor need to tell her of all the interesting things that had happened thus far on the cruise. There would be time enough for that once we were safely home in Norfolk. Things at home were fine according to her, and being the fine navy wife she was I knew our home was in safe hands. It had been an interesting stay in Port Lytteton and Christ Church, and now it was time for Wyandot to begin the journey back to Norfolk. The ship's boilers had been cleaned and the black gang had worked hard to accomplish this. The ship had been refueled and all preparations were made to get underway. On 26 January, 1959, the special sea detail was set and Wyandot was once again underway; this time her first stop would be in Auckland, New Zealand on North Island. It was only a two day cruise and the ship arrived on 28 January.

The vibrations caused by the bent blade on the screw continued and of course, the maximum speed was always rung up on the engine room enunciator. The vibration seemed to amplify as it traveled through the ship and culminated at the forward tripod mast. One could stand at the foot of the mast and feel and see the vibration as it traveled to the top of the mast. My main concern was that the weld that held the mast to the deck would not crack as a result of the constant vibration. I would check this many times each day and night on our journey home.

The weather, on our arrival in Auckland, was foul and raining. I was not impressed with the surroundings and had no desire to go ashore. However, on the second day in port a tour bus was hired to take a few of the crew to Rotarura; this was a National Park similar to our Yellowstone National Park. Once in Rotarura the group could visit a Native Maori village. This appeared to be an interesting trip and I decided to go with the group. On our way to the park, the bus stopped at a hydroelectric power dam, and we were allowed a short visit of the site. The New Zealand bus driver was extremely proud of this dam and exhorted all its qualities to any who would listen.

In the meantime, the rain had increased and I had no desire to get off the bus once we arrived at Rotarura. One of the group was a Chaplain who had wintered over at McMurdo and was returning to the states as a passenger on the Wyandot. During his winter stay in the Antarctic, he had grown a very full black beard, which he continued to sport on his voyage home. On our arrival, noting that I was not going to get off the bus for the tour, he asked if he could borrow my uniform khaki raincoat. I was hesitant to lend it to him, but did not have the nerve to say no. There were a few of the group that also had no desire to get out in the rain, so we bided our time with idle talk and eating the lunch that had been provided by the ship's cooks.

The tour took about an hour and the group returned wet to the bone. The chaplain, who had borrowed my coat, returned it with a guilty look on his face. During the tour, he had partaken of a mug of coffee, which he spilled in his full black beard and it ran down on my raincoat. The coffee had left a large stain on the front of the coat, and I was never able to get it removed. He never offered to rectify the damage, so much for Chaplains.

The trip had given us the opportunity to get away from the ship for a few hours and from our seats on the bus, we were able to view the walls of the native village, which were made of small trees much like an American Indian stockade. Rotarura is volcanic in nature and one could see beyond the village walls the rising steam from the hot springs that abound. All in all, it had been interesting, even with my limited visit. The trip back to the ship was a quiet ride; it was good to be back on board again. On the third day of our visit, 31 January, 1959 we got underway for Sydney, Australia.

Our route to Sydney charted the ship around North Cape and Cape Maria at the northern tip of North Island. We arrived at Sydney on 4 February, 1959 and dropped anchor in the inner harbor near the Sydney Bridge. The constant thumping of the unbalanced ship's screw during the trip continued, as well as my worried concern of the consequences. I had posted an additional watch in the shaft alley, a compartment through which the shaft passed to its connection with the main engine. The shaft was supported in this compartment by several large main bearings, and I was concerned that one or more of these bearings could become overheated because of the unbalanced screw. The bearings are normally lubricated by a yarn wick that drips oil from a small reservoir on the bearing to the bearing surface. The added watch made sure there was a man there at all times to assure there was adequate lubrication. Normally the watch in the engine room would make a frequent check of the shaft alley and check the bearings. So far, there was no indication that any of the bearings were overheating, but the long voyage that lie ahead might present a problem. During this transit, the Captain had not questioned me one time about the performance of the damaged screw; it was as if nothing had happened.

Sydney Harbor is a beautiful one and it was a welcome sight after the gloominess of Auckland and its rainy weather. One could see the Sydney Opera House, with its impressive architecture, that was under construction. The word we received was they stopped construction; due to insufficient revenue from the lottery, these funds were for the project. In time, of course, it was completed. It is known worldwide for its beauty and quaint design. The weather was perfect, with sunshine, blue skies, and a very pleasant temperature. Officers of the Australian Navy welcomed us and host officers had been assigned to show us around the city. It was a very nice welcome for all of us.

It was mid-summer in Australia and the weather was perfect our entire visit. The ship's anchorage in the bay provided an excellent view of the city, and with some of my shipmates, I visited several of the sites. The trip to Bondi Beach was enjoyable, although I never ventured into the water for a swim. A good deal of my time was involved with making sure the Engineering Department was prepared for the month long journey back to Norfolk. On the visits ashore, I enjoyed the Australian beer; I shall always remember the taste of a pint of Fosters. The name of my Australian counterpart, who had been assigned to accompany me ashore, I must admit I have long forgotten, but he was a gracious host. Our stay in port lasted six days when once again we set sail for home.

The special sea detail set, we cleared the harbor and set our course slightly southeast to pass through Cook Strait, which took us between New Zealand's North and South Islands. Once clear of the strait our course changed to northeast and the long voyage to Panama began. The thump, thump of the unbalanced damaged screw increased with our speed, which was rung up on the engine order telegraph at Flank Speed. There was to be no change in the Captain's desire to get all the speed he could have us muster come hell or high water. The message I had drafted to report our damage, and which had not been released, was kept in my safe in my quarters. This was my only defense should the ship sustain further damage, as a consequence of the damaged propeller, as we steamed home to Norfolk. My long watch would involve many hours of constant vigilance and frequent checks of the vibrating forward tripod mast and the main engines and boilers. I had learned a long time ago that trouble usually occurred when one least expected it. My Main Propulsion Officer, Warrant Machinist Douglas, shared the same concern and anxiety as I, and disbelief that the Captain would not release my damage report message.

The daily routine at sea can and does become increasingly monotonous. The daily watches and work schedule fall slowly into place, and the rolling motion of the ship lulls one into a rather listless stupor. You get used to the many ship's noises, the creaking of the rigging, the steady hum of the ventilation blowers, the subdued voices of the crew, and the increasing temperature as the ship entered the tropical zone. The best description is organized boredom. The stretch of ocean that lay ahead seemed endless, and Panama a distant goal of relief. Looking aft, one viewed the wake of the ship; if one traced it, it became a watery rope that bound you to Antarctica from whence we came.

Day after day, we steamed east by northeast; my concern for the vibration never slackened. The temperature in the engineering spaces continued to rise; every piece of piping, machinery or metal within arms reach was so hot it burned your hand at its touch. The steaming at Flank Speed required the boilers to be fired at one hundred and twenty percent in order to maintain the speed the Captain wanted. This figure I determined by the rate of fuel consumption of the oil fired boilers. One good event was the continuing success of the jury-rigged ventilation of the electric forced draft blower motors, which had been implemented after the earlier failure at the beginning of the cruise. The ducting of outside air to the motors had kept the soot and stack gas leaking from the boiler casing from contaminating the motor windings. Even though it seemed to be working I never felt completely at ease, and thus I added that to my numerous rounds of inspection.

Two weeks of steaming at Flank Speed had passed, when I was informed that one of the hand hole gaskets in the super-heater header on number two boiler was leaking. This was bad news for such a leak continued to increase with time. I made my way to the bridge and requested permission to enter to see the Captain. He was sitting in his chair at the railing on the bridge when I presented him with the newest problem. He asked the severity of the leak and I told him the leak was considerable and asked permission to take number two boiler off the line and let it cool for repairs. He asked would the leak increase; I told him it would. His reply, "we will steam another day", and to let him know the next morning what the situation was at that time". I told him it would only get worse, but he declined my request to secure the boiler. I left the bridge and went below to the Engineering Log room, where I called Warrant Officer Douglas and told him what the Captain had ordered. He in turn told me the leak would only get worse, and I concurred. I told him the Captain had been so advised.

The heat in the engine room and fire room was intense, coupled with the ship's position at the time in the equatorial region, and the escaping steam from the boiler leak. I knew that once my men were allowed to commence repairs that the working conditions would be difficult. The men in the boiler watch continued to monitor the leak as I did. It was obvious that the leak was gradually getting worse; the sound of the escaping superheated steam verified that. The night wore on and sometime after midnight I turned in for some rest. I continued to ponder the question of why the Captain would not agree to secure the boiler and prepare it for repairs. According to the navigator, the ship was well ahead of its intended track of advance. Our arrival date back in Norfolk was not operationally fixed; it had to be some inner force driving the Captain to fulfill some personal goal.

Dawn came early in the tropics and reluctantly I rubbed the sleep from my eyes and dressed for the day ahead. My first chore was to evaluate the situation with the boiler leak, and as predicted, it had increased. At 0800, I made my way to the bridge and informed the Captain, as he had directed me to do the day before, that the leak was worse.

Once again, I requested permission to secure the boiler and take it off the line for repair. Reluctantly he granted my request, and as I departed the bridge, I could hear the order to reduce speed given to the Officer of the Deck. I directed Warrant Officer Douglas to secure the fires under number two boiler, and to begin repairs when it had cooled sufficiently. This was at approximately 0830; at 1030, I was summoned to the bridge and he asked me how repairs were progressing. I informed him that the boiler was still too hot to open it for work, that it was still forming steam from the residual heat. It would take some time before it was cool enough for my men to work.

I stood there for what seemed a long time waiting for his reply; it was just seconds, when he told me to blow the boiler down and start repairs. I could not believe what I heard; we had been steaming two weeks at Flank Speed, with the air temperature increasing every day. As we approached the equator, the heat increased. The engineering spaces became very hot where my men would have to work. A boiler under those circumstances did not cool in a matter of a couple of hours. I told the Captain if I blew the boiler down, without allowing it to cool naturally that it was highly possible we could sustain additional problems. I also informed him that it would be extremely difficult for my men to work on a boiler that was still emitting steam. His response was, "Mr. Hamelrath you are far too conservative, blow that boiler down." I replied, "Aye, Aye Captain," and left the bridge.

It is essential at this point in this story to say that all the incidents involving sustained damage, orders from the Captain that contradicted proper engineering procedures, and action taken by engineering personnel at the direction of my orders was entered in the Engineering Log. This is standard action in accordance with regulations. The Captain is required to review and sign the Log after I had signed it. On numerous occasions, he would not sign it until I had modified the entry to his satisfaction. He could not or would not accept the fact that he was instrumental to the cause of the damage, because of his orders.

After leaving the bridge, I informed Warrant Officer Douglas that the Captain had ordered me to blow down number two boiler and commence repairs. With grave reluctance, he complied. It took some time before this was accomplished, but upon completion the boiler crew started to remove the leaking hand hole cover. It was immediately evident that steam was still being generated as a cloud of it blew out in the faces of the men doing the work. Air hoses from the air compressor had to be used to blow the escaping steam away so the men could continue their repairs. The area in which the men had to work was restricted, because the after bulkhead of the boiler room was only about two feet from the back of the boiler. It was a tight space in which to work and the extreme heat posed a problem of possible heat exhaustion for the men.

The leaking steam had cut the gasket surface of the hand hole; this would have to be welded and then ground to a smooth surface before a new gasket could be installed. Normal procedure requires that only a certified welder for high-pressure welds can do the work. There were no certified welders available so I picked the one that was considered our best. The welding was important and had to be done slowly and precisely, but the time consuming part of the repair was the grinding and smoothing of the weld. Frequent rotation of the men working had to be done because of the stifling heat. The hours passed by and frequent trips to the bridge kept the Captain informed of the progress.

At approximately 2200 (10:00 PM) repairs were near completion when someone, because of the tight working area, stepped on a drain valve at the base of the boiler and it broke loose. This required another welding job, which delayed repairs. I again informed the Captain. My boiler gang had been on the job for twelve hours, working in some of the most difficult conditions, and I was not surprised that there had not been other mishaps. Fortunately, the welding of the broken valve did not take a long time, and at last, I was able to tell the fire room watch to light fires under the boiler in preparation to bringing the boiler back on the line. The Engineering Officer of the Watch was told to inform the bridge that repairs had been completed and we were lighting fires under number two boiler.

It was near midnight, 2400 navy time, when I made my way up to the bridge to inform the Captain that number two boiler was back on the line and that we were increasing the main engines RPM to Flank Speed. I was extremely tired and frustrated from the long hours that had taxed my mental and physical strength. The forced deviation from the sound engineering practices that I had learned over the years, and the obvious bypassing of regulations in reporting mechanical casualties, had contributed to my condition. The blackness of the night was broken as I entered the dimly lighted wheelhouse of the bridge. The Captain's outline could be seen as he sat in his chair. I reported to him, saluted, and informed him personally we were coming back up to speed. He answered curtly, that he knew that, then in a gruff and abusing loud voice that all could hear, he remarked, "Well Mr. Hamelrath are all of your boiler problems over for the rest of the cruise?" With that, he rose and left the bridge for his cabin.

I followed him as he left the bridge and descended the ladder that lead down to the deck level of his cabin. His last remark had set my brain in a whirl, a rush of strange thoughts overcame me and as I followed him down the ladder, I reached a point of inner uncontrollable rage. I was very close behind him, I do not know if he was aware of my presence or not. My thoughts were what if I threw him overboard; we were close to the ship's railing. Could I throw him far enough to miss the ready lifeboat, which was dimly visible hanging in the davit on the starboard side. This thought passed as quickly as it had materialized in my brain, and I grasped the handrail at the ship's side and squeezed it until my hands hurt, all the time telling myself to get yourself in order. I had never in my life been so close to losing it; I stood there in the darkness for quite some time, and when at last composed I went to my cabin and turned in.

I arose the next morning somewhat refreshed, the actions that I had contemplated mentally the night before had now become a bad memory. I was ashamed that I had let strife undo me as it had. The long hours and mechanical problems I was used to were all part of my responsibility as the ship's Engineering Office. The disregard for regulations and proper procedures was what tipped the scales, and I would never regain respect for the Captain.

The boiler repairs were completed and we were now six days out of Panama. The continual thump, thump of the damaged screw had become routine, but my anxiety remained and would until the cruise was completed. I was still concerned that the weld at the forward cargo boom mast might fail from fatigue due to the vibrations. Frequent inspections continued during the entire homeward cruise. It was about this time that the word was going around that the ship would be decommissioned on our return to Norfolk. I was never informed directly that this was correct, but the actions that followed confirmed that it was true. The first instructions the Department Heads received was to commence an inventory of all equipment and repair parts in their area of responsibility.

On the second day, after giving the order to inventory all items, the Gunnery Department reported that a Colt 45 Caliber Semi-automatic pistol was missing. We knew the weapon was onboard, but who had it was the question. The Captain gave the order to form search parties, and a thorough search of the ship would be conducted if the pistol were not returned. I was assigned several personnel and to conduct my search of the Que Sera Sera, which was the plane we were carrying. As mentioned earlier it was a Navy R4D, the one Admiral Byrd had flown to the South Pole. It was being returned to be displayed at the Naval Aviation Museum in Pensacola, Florida Naval Station. The gun was not returned so the search began.

The plane fuselage had been insulated with panels that could be removed, which is what my crew had to do. There was any number of places the gun could have been hidden, besides behind the insulating panels. The search took several hours and in the end, the results were negative. The results were the same with all the other search parties. The pistol could not be found, so the Captain passed the word there would be no liberty for the crew when the ship reaches Panama. If the weapon were still missing, the Naval Investigative Service would be advised. A short time later, the weapon was mysteriously found. Where it was found was never disclosed and the culprit remained unknown. This incident caused quite a stir amongst the crew, mainly because there would have been no liberty once the ship reached Panama. No liberty is always a sore spot with any crew, and the Wyandot was no exception.

On 3 March, 1959, after three weeks of steady steaming from Sydney, the ship reached Panama. It had been a long trip and no other ships or land had been sighted the entire time. The continuous worry involved with the damaged screw, the boiler problems, and the over firing of the boilers, had kept me working near my limit. No one was happier than I was when we finally reached our last stop before Norfolk. The officers and crew enjoyed the three days the ship was in port. I remained onboard and relaxed in the solitude of my room.

On 6 March, after three steamy hot days in Panama the special sea detail was set, the canal pilot came on board and Wyandot began the last leg of its journey. The ship entered the canal for its return crossing to the Atlantic. The trip through the canal was uneventful, and in due time the Isthmus of Panama faded astern, Wyandot was now in home waters and Norfolk bound. On 9 March, Cape Henry was sighted and the ship entered Chesapeake Bay. Hampton Roads and the Naval Base lie ahead and our journey to the Antarctic and back was about to end. The ship had steamed 2,500 more nautical miles than the distance around the world. At this point, I did not know that yet another chapter was about to begin before the cruise was really over. My main thought at this time was my wife, Rose, and daughter, Linda, to see them again after the past long months were all that was important. There was much they had to tell me after my absence, but I had a tale to tell as well.

Rose met me when the ship docked and it was a very happy moment. All the trials and worries of the past few months faded when once again we were in each other's arms. Linda, our daughter would join us when the school day was over. She had grown while I was away and was maturing into a lovely young lady. I had purchased a few gifts on the journey and these were passed out. The nicest one I think was a Merino sheep pelt that had been made into a throw rug. This was for the floor by the bed; a nice thing to step on in ones bare feet. During our reunion as a family, I related all the stories of the cruise, which would be amplified with all the pictures and movies I had taken, once they were developed.

It was now official the Wyandot would be decommissioned in Orange, Texas. This was the Naval Station where many decommissioned ships were held in reserve status for any future recall to duty. In the meantime, the ship was undergoing pre-decommissioning procedures. Equipment that was in excess or not required for readiness was made available to other ships of the Service Force Atlantic Fleet, of which Wyandot was assigned. Leave was also granted to members of the crew. I was granted a ten day leave, which my family enjoyed.

Prior to my departure on leave, I had instructed my oil king, a boiler Technician First Class, to pump our surplus fuel oil to the barge that would come alongside, while I was away. We had instructions to transfer all but ten percent of our oil, this would allow the ship to float high enough for its trip up the shallow Sabine River to Orange, Texas. A problem would develop later, on the ship's voyage to Texas, when sea water ballast that had been added to the supposedly empty fuel tanks was pumped out. Ballast had to be added for the trip to replace the oil that had been transferred to the fuel barge. This would provide adequate draft for the ship's screw to perform properly, although it was still bent out of alignment.

It was late in April when all preparations were completed for Wyandot's departure for decommissioning in Orange, Texas. Our time in port with our families was short lived, and it was time to set the Special Sea Detail again. I said my goodbye to Rose and Linda, which was always a difficult time, and once again was underway. Once in Orange, Texas the ship would have sixty days in which to prepare for deactivation. That was a tight schedule for all the work that would have to be accomplished, but my absence from home would be short lived.

The trip down to the Gulf of Mexico was uneventful, and up until this time, I had never been assigned an underway deck watch. As Chief Engineer and a Department Head, my routine duties had exempted me from such watches. My appointment as a commissioned officer was Limited Duty Engineering, but I had requested to be qualified as an underway deck officer when I reported to my first ship after commissioning. The Captain granted my request, so my service record included this qualification. I assume that on this basis the Captain included me on the underway watch officer's list. My one and only assigned watch was after we entered the gulf, and it would give me an unwanted surprise.

It was at this time that the Engineering Department was ordered to pump the seawater water ballast we had taken on in Norfolk to replace the fuel oil we had off loaded. It was time to decrease our draft for our trip up the shallow Sabine River to Orange. I passed the order to my oil king and soon after the pumping started. From my position on the bridge, I was able to look aft, and instead of a stream of salt water a steady stream of fuel oil drifted into the wake of the ship. I immediately ordered the pumping be stopped and passed the word for my oil king to report to me. I asked him why we were getting fuel oil from a tank that was supposed to hold only salt water. His answer explained it all, instead of sounding the tanks when the excess fuel was off loaded he merely pumped until the pump lost suction and then moved on to another tank. The pumps, I figured lost suction because the oil at the time of off-loading was too cold for the pumps to handle. When the fuel oil pumps lost suction, the oil king thought the tanks were empty The fuel oil tank heaters leaked too badly to heat the oil. If they were used, they allowed fuel oil to enter the heating coils, which eventually contaminated the condensed steam drain system. That was my surprise, I did not like it, and I expressed my feelings to my oil king in a very determined manner. This had all taken place while I had been on my short leave in Norfolk, and in spite of that, I still felt responsible. Now my big concern was, is that added ballast going to increase the maximum draft allowed for the ship to be safely towed up the Sabine River to Orange. For once good fortune was on my side and it did not pose any problem.

Traversing the Gulf of Mexico to the entrance to the Sabine River was interesting. While I was on my watch on the bridge numerous sightings of contacts were made on radar, but most of them were oil rigs pumping oil from the depths of the gulf. Man had made a tremendous step in technology for extracting our much needed fuel. This was my first experience in viewing the rigs and I was amazed.

At last, Wyandot reached the entrance to the Sabine River and proceeded to Port Arthur, where the ship docked. I ordered the main engines and boilers for the last time, and workers came on board and welded braces to the propeller shaft. This was necessary so the shaft would not revolve during our towed trip to Orange. With no power, available lubricating oil to the main engine reduction gears was not available. Without lubrication, bearings could be damaged if the main engine shaft revolved, because of the current in the Sabine River during Wyandot's towed journey by tug to Orange.

The morning after the workers had completed their securing of the main engine shaft, tugs came alongside and cast their lines to our deck crew, and Wyandot began her trip up the river to the Naval Base at Orange, Texas. A river pilot had come on board to pilot the ship on its journey. It was a very quiet departure, the only sound of ship activity was the muffled noise of the ship's emergency diesel generator, which provided the basic electrical power for the ship. The normal ship activity had ceased and the almost utter silence had a rather sad effect. For all normal purposes, the ship was lifeless, and I stood at the ships railing and watched in silence as the shoreline slipped slowly and quietly astern. The past few months had presented a strange transition for me, from a new assignment to a challenging journey to the southern end of the globe, and now a quiet trip to decommissioning. In my mind I would ponder for a long time all the troubling situations to which I had been associated. I had yet to figure out the thinking and behavior of the Captain.

The sound of the tug's engines slowed and Orange, Texas came into view. Skillfully they maneuvered Wyandot into her anchorage off the Naval Base, and her anchor let go for the final time. The tugs cast off their lines and the ship came to rest in the current of the Sabine River. Although it was still May, the air was hot and humid, the slowly moving river with its muddy current provided no relief. It was obvious the next two months of decommissioning would be uncomfortable, moving the ship's crew ashore might provide them some comfort. Prior to that, we would receive our decommissioning syllabus. This contained all the correct procedures for deactivating and preserving the ship's machinery and systems.

Shortly after our arrival, the Captain reported to the base Commodore, as required by navy regulations. The Commodore, a navy captain, was a Naval Academy classmate of the Wyandot's Captain and a few numbers senior to him. Shortly thereafter, base personnel came onboard. They would inspect and instruct our sailors on the decommissioning procedures. At this time, we found out that Wyandot would be decommissioned and her machinery and systems preserved using a wet process rather than the airtight method used on most combat vessels. All piping systems and all machinery would be drained and filled with an oil preservative. All surfaces below deck would be sprayed with the same agent. Electrical motors and equipment would be opened, cleaned and sprayed with an antifungal agent. It was obvious that this would be a time consuming task and it would have to be done within two months. Most of the systems fell within the responsibility of the Engineering Department, as the other departments had little to preserve.

The next day work began on the preliminary items. My responsibility included reviewing all work requests submitted by other department heads for repair work that would be required to make the ship seaworthy if it should be commissioned again in the future. The number of work requests for the Engineering Department alone would be staggering, and would number in the hundreds when once completed. All hands were eager to get started, for no one looked forward to two months in Orange, Texas with the heat and humidity as they were. All of this enthusiasm was curtailed when the Captain assembled all the ship's officers in the wardroom and announced the following; "Gentlemen, the ship is now in a very particular and different set of circumstances so all ship's bills will be rewritten and adjusted to these new conditions."

We were astonished to say the least that all work we had started on the decommissioning must be stopped. This order meant the fire bill, man overboard bill, general quarters bill, abandon ship bill, collision bill, and all bills would be rewritten. Once again our Captain was going against the tide, so to speak. The prime reason for the ship being in Orange, Texas was pushed aside so his whims could be fulfilled. The fact that the ship was as dead as an empty barge did not seem to register with him. As soon as space became available Wyandot would be moved from her anchorage in the river to a dock at the Naval Base. Once this was accomplished work would begin in earnest to meet our deadline. It did not take long for the word about this delay reached the Commodore. The Captain was henceforth summoned to the Commodore's office.

Wyandot was moved dockside the next day and work resumed on decommissioning the ship. At this time I had no idea that in the very near future there would be a change in my field of responsibility. Within the week a set of orders arrived for the Captain as well as for me. The Captain was detached and I was ordered as his relief. The change of command ceremony was held a few days later on the dock. By this time all hands had moved ashore to the base barracks, the living conditions aboard ship no longer existed. The ceremony should have been short and uneventful, but there always had to be something just a bit different with our Captain. The Captain read his orders and then I read mine, at which time I said, "I relieve you sir." I said this in the normal speaking voice which was audible to all I was sure, but not for the Captain. He stopped the proceedings and told me to say again, "I relieve you sir", and to shout loudly, so all could hear. I was embarrassed, but I had no choice but to comply. With that we saluted and he departed shortly thereafter. I was now in command of a ship that could go nowhere, but at least now we could get on with the business we had been sent here to do.

I had moved ashore to the Bachelor's Officers Quarters, which turned out to be a very sparsely furnished room. There was no air conditioning as this was still a time of limited niceties, air conditioning being one of them. I had managed to acquire an electric fan and a refrigerator. I was in hog heaven as luxuries go, and I could keep some food in my room for snacks and for lunch. I avoided the mess hall for economical reasons as I was on a limited budget. The one area that had air conditioning was the small bar that served cold beer. I would spend evenings there to keep cool before retiring to my room for the night.

Work aboard ship continued and Chief Warrant Machinist Douglas, my main assistant, kept the ball rolling. My duties now consisted of supervising the overall progress of decommissioning as well as performing the duties of Commanding Officer. This was limited now to exercising disciplinary action when required, maintaining the ship's log and diary, and signing transfer orders of personnel when their duties had been completed in their departments' area. There was still the ongoing preparation of a file of necessary work requests for the ship if it was ordered for reactivation. This all fell within my realm of responsibility as the Engineering Officer. Once the work list had been compiled, it was amazing the work that would have to be accomplished to ready Wyandot for sea again.

Each day, as I made my rounds aboard ship checking the progress of work, I found it was becoming more difficult to tour the ship safely, especially the engineering spaces. The preservative oil that was being applied to all interior piping and exposed areas made everything exceedingly slippery. One had to be exceptionally cautious so he would not slip, fall and suffer an injury. Fortunately this did not happen to anyone and we completed the work without anyone being hurt. The constant heat and high humidity also contributed to the very uncomfortable environment. It was now mid -June and each day these elements continued to increase.

One by one the different systems of the ship were preserved and noted in my daily progress report. One day warrant Officer Douglas and a couple of his men brought an item to my office for display. During our sojourn through the ice in the Antarctic our Captain had religiously sounded the ship's horn whenever a course change was made, as required by Rules of The Road. He would do this even if the Wyandot were the only ship present. This always provided humor to the crew and we often wondered what the occasional penguin thought when it was sounded. Perhaps that is why we saw so few when we were underway. The item the men had brought for me to see was the diaphragm in the ship's horn. It was made of bronze and the constant, frequent blasting had cracked the diaphragm from one edge to the other. We all laughed and decided we were the first ones to wear out a ship's horn. Fortunately there was a spare diaphragm available and a repair was made on site. This was one item, which would not require a work order to be placed in the file.

Going on shore leave was not an especially inviting event. Orange did not offer much in the way of entertainment, but there was one place I always enjoyed visiting. Mr. Douglas had been in Orange before and he knew of an excellent place to get good southern barbecue. There was a little place run by a black man; it was open on all sides but capable of being closed at night with large shutters. The place had about six small tables, which were covered by immaculate red and white checkered table cloths. The barbecue pit, which was wood fired, was located inside. The fire pit was outside and the heat from the fire was fed to the barbecue grill by a long tunnel. The operation was very efficient and the food absolutely mouth-watering. The barbecued pork would melt in your mouth, and a glass of good cold buttermilk added much to the meal. During my time in Orange I made several trips there, each time I came away completely satisfied.

As Commanding Officer I only had a few disciplinary cases. These were mainly men who were late getting back from liberty. I held Captain's Mast as prescribed by the Uniform Code of Military Justice. In all cases I prescribed restriction to the base for a short period, to be suspended on good behavior. The penalty was not entered into their records and there were no following violations. The size of the crew continued to diminish as the work progressed. Most of the officers had been transferred and the engineering department personnel remained the largest onboard force. Periodically I would make my required report of progress to the Base Commodore, Captain Sampson. He was a fine gentleman and it was a pleasure to work for him.

The tenth of July, 1959 was the target date for decommissioning. One by one each shipboard system was checked, and at last, the final inspection by the base crew was completed. The decommissioning ceremony was to be held on the dock, and at last, the day and time arrived. All hands that remained were anxious to leave the area and get on with their new duty assignments. I think I headed that list. The ceremony was brief; the colors were lowered and were properly folded. The commissioning pennant was handed to me, which I kept for years as my reminder of a ship I once Captained, but could never sail. I gave the ship one last long look as I walked from the dock.

I had served in her for less than a year, but in that time it seemed I encountered a lifetime of stress and experience. I was sure I was leaving as a better officer and a man.

The crew and I said our goodbyes and they all departed. I gathered all the items required to be delivered to the Commodore and took them to his office. We chatted briefly and then I made my way to my quarters. There was something that had been pending for many months and now I was about to do it. The messages that I had drafted, but never released by the Commanding Officer, to The Bureau of Ships and Commander Service Force Atlantic Fleet reporting our material casualties while in the Antarctic were still in my file. I removed these and destroyed them. The final act of my continued discomfort of not being able to abide by Navy Regulations was completed. I would live with these memories for the rest of my life.

Chief Warrant Officer Douglas and I both agreed it had been an exceptional tour of duty. We had formed a definite bond because of sharing dubious feelings about our former Captain. With our luggage, we headed for the Greyhound Bus Depot. We shared a ride as far as Charleston, South Carolina, where we parted. He to his next duty station, and I on to Norfolk, Virginia where I would report as Staff Material Officer of Amphibious Squadron Ten.

Before leaving the dock, after the ceremonies, I took the time to share a few minutes of my memories of the past months in the Wyandot. I looked back at the now silent ship, just a ghost, silent, empty of human occupancy, a hull filled with memories of a strange man. In no way is this intended to criticize the actions of the Captain, as Commanding Officer it was his prerogative to analyze situations as he saw them and issue orders accordingly.

I had at last formed my opinion of what drove that man, our Captain, to sometimes strange behavior. He was at heart an actor, a man searching for popular acceptance He was born two hundred years too late. He wanted to be a man of adventure, a man of history, a man of exploration. His brief acquaintance with Sir Raymond Priestley, our Antarctic Explorer passenger, only exacerbated this unfulfilled desire. His role as Captain John Smith, his deviation from the ordinary required procedures, his mountain climbing when he should have been tending his ship, this all pointed to a man with frustrated desires for recognition. As for his persistent driving the ship at Flank Speed, I feel it was a rationalization of a desire to be remembered, in the same vein as Captain Arleigh Burke. Captain Burke was known during World War II as 31 knot Burke. He was a Destroyer Division Commander and always proceeded at 31 knots when on a sortie to engage the enemy. Our Captain had to be different, this was the force that drove him in his attempt to make his mark in history. In later years after my retirement from the navy, we would meet socially but he never mentioned or discussed our months together in Wyandot.

Foot Note: In early 1961, while serving as Staff Material Officer of Amphibious Squadron Ten, I received a copy of a message stating, Wyandot would be activated and assigned to our squadron. This meant I would once again be involved with her materiel problems. I informed our Commodore that I had been her Engineering Officer, put her out off-commission, and knew her materiel situation, and the amount of work that would have to be accomplished to put her back in commission. The Commodore advised me to write a letter to the prospective commanding officer and explain Wyandot's condition. I complied, but never received an answer; however, Wyandot was not reactivated for the navy. She was put in service for the navy with a civilian crew. The cost of reactivating her was passed to a different source of funds, probably saving the navy a good deal of money.

PART III OPINIONS

Political Thoughts

The following articles are political in nature. They have drawn criticism from several readers, when they were published in the local newspaper. I served my country in the military from 1938 until 1970 when I retired from active duty. During that time, I swore allegiance to numerous presidents and always pledged myself to obey and carry out all orders of those appointed over me, including the Commander In Chief. That pledge did not require me to accept the political posture or beliefs of the man who held the office of the president. I have taken great exception to the administration of Barack Obama and the direction he is leading the nation. My articles fully express my thoughts and beliefs on this subject.

Published in the Coeur d' Alene, Idaho Press March 27, 2010

The "Question" of Change

I am eighty-eight years old, I was born in the aftermath of World War I. Since that time I have witnessed many changes, some good, and some bad. I have seen nations rise and fall, Germany, Russia, Italy, China and North Korea to name a few. Their demise was caused by turmoil from within, not from the final battles, but from human ideology that started at leadership level. This ideology was called "change", and it came in many forms, most of it designed to sell to the public mind. It did not matter if the public understood the "change"; it was just important that it was "change".

As far back as I can remember change has taken place, as a result, in many cases, the nation and the people benefited. In other instances, they have not. For decades, our Congressional Bodies have effected changes that have quietly and subtly built a hierarchy, which has removed them from the laws of the common man. No one needs to approve of a pay raise except that Royal body; they receive a retirement after one term of office, and this extends to their spouse. They have their own health plan; they do not contribute to Social Security. They accept bribes from lobbyists and their own peers, you vote for my pork and I will vote for yours. They operate under their own set of rules; if a new member does not play by their game, he never gets to achieve much, regardless of his well-intended ideas. The list goes on.

This nation exists because our forefathers fought a war of independence to remove themselves from such practices. Government was to be the same for all people. Respect for elected officials was earned not granted. This was the lesson my classmates and I was taught, back when current events, civics, and history became the foundation for our national patriotism. I well remember following events occurring in Germany under Hitler, and Italy under Mussolini, and saying this can never happen here.

Today I am not so sure. Everywhere I turn I continue to find people who do not know history, do not know that history tends to repeat itself when the public becomes less informed, apathetic or simply do not think mistakes made by nations in the past are relevant. I am deeply concerned by our current administration. The current President has no patriotic toes to our nation. His agenda appears to be personal and not of the nation.

His "change" is to take place whatever the consequences. Changes, if needed at all, cannot be implemented by committee or a timetable, without analyzing closely the consequences of such change. The purpose of government is to lead not control. Capitalism developed this nation; it has its problems, and at times, it loses sight of morality, which you cannot legislate. Greed will rear its ugly head no matter what. There are those who forget you can only live in one house or sleep in one bed at a time.

Sadly, governmental change can take place if we fail to pay attention to plans that are proposed to take care of all the needy ones. I am addressing this to those who would use the goodness of nation to their own best advantage without contributing to its existence. A welfare state will lead to Socialism, and a nation of our size and population will decay. Handout government will appeal too many and it will, because of its existence generate a popular and controlling vote. This is the idea behind many changes that may be offered. Do not for one instant think this cannot happen. Hitler knew, and a nation blindly followed him. With that thought, I propose a change.

In the very near future, we will be going to the polls to cast our votes for members of Congress. This will be the time for "people" to effect change. It is time we elect men or women who will implement the change to remove one of the most corrupting aspects of our legislative bodies. Vote for someone who will vow to remove the element of "privilege" from our houses of government. Privilege corrupts; the Land of Oz living, that our legislators abide in, needs to come down. If you do not vote out the pig trough, the new pig will soon adjust to the good living. Remove the trough and the pig will get in line with the rest of us. This may be overly simplistic, but our legislators need to get the word. It is time "public servant" again becomes the banner for our representatives of government to hoist and to carry proudly for a nation that was once the greatest and most respected in the world. There was a time when a person running for public office did so with the conviction that he or she had something worthy to offer to the office, not what the office would provide for them. John Adams, one of the finest of our founding fathers, was adamantly against party politics. He knew the dangers of party affiliation and its affliction. No one would listen, and politics became party oriented. No one party has ever had all the correct answers to the nation's problems.

There is one more change that could remove the earmarks and pork that frequently are applied to our bills of legislation. An amendment should be made to the Constitution stating that no amendment or rider can be attached to a bill unless it pertains exclusively to the basic bill. If a matter of expenditure is of such consequence, that is essential to a cause then it should be able to stand on its own merit, and not sneaked in on the shirttail of another and sometimes very important bill, which is frequently done with the Defense Department's Appropriations Bill. The moneys that could be saved on such an amendment are beyond comprehension. If our Legislative Bodies were to do this then we would know some real and proper change was taking place, but don't hold your breath, this makes too much sense to ever happen.

I am genuinely and gravely concerned with the immediate future of our country. At the present rate of fraud, misuse of public funds, governmental control of industry, and now the health of the nation, fiscal solvency of the nation could dissolve overnight. We are on the brink of a dark chasm of uncertainty, with no solid bridge on which to cross.

I wish to speak on behalf of all the veterans, who in my lifetime stood and defended, many times at the offering of their very lives, the cause of this once great nation. At age sixteen, proudly patriotic, I joined The Idaho National Guard; at eighteen, I joined the Navy and served for thirty years. I have never lost my love for my country. My most profound hope is none of us served in vain. God Bless all of you, and may this once proud nation survive with its head held high.

Foot note:

This article was written approximately four years ago, and the situation in our country is now more uncertain than it was at that time. Our president's agenda now seems to be more solidified. His intent seems to be the total destruction of the nation's financial institution, government control of all agencies that affect the general welfare and health of its citizens, and his consistent attempt to redistribute the wealth of the successful people in our society. The economy of the nation cannot be sustained without hardworking wage earners; simple mathematics will tell and verify that you have to put in before there is anything to take out. He has surrounded himself with a hierarchy of self- appointed Czars, which operate much as he dictates.

This is Marxist and the public needs to realize this. The president is an astute student of psychology, and he applies it very well. He gained his political foothold as a community organizer, where one can build a political base of future voters. One only needs to tell the people what they want to hear, and he does this very well. He has no problem contradicting himself on previous statements if his recent proclamations are more to his advantage. He knows people tend to remember more of what they last heard if it sounds better to them. This is more of his knowledge of psychology. The president has no background of prior achievements as a senator or as a private citizen. This man is a "sleeper" cast in our midst from a very shadowy past. He has created enough political and financial chaos that will be with us for decades to come. He has accomplished this "job" in four years; he does not need a second term. Why the Democratic Party continues to travel down this road with him is beyond comprehension.

Published in the Coeur d' Alene, Idaho Press August 27, 2010

A Proposition for Review

This article is submitted as a proposition for review, and consideration, by all people of voting age, who will take the time to read it. Our nation is being constantly assailed, physically as well as ideologically and religiously. Our borders are but a sieve for illegal immigrants, our social structure is being undermined by wide spread drug use, our political structure has strayed from true representation to a special interest agenda. The list can go on, but there has to be a stand taken somewhere to mend the national degradation.

I am sure there are many who are aware of this decline in our nation's stature, and in their own way try to counter it. Many do not; they either do not know what is happening, they think subtle change is not taking place, they do not view what is happening as important and real, are blatantly apathetic, or frankly they do not give a damn.

Recently there has been strong opposition to the building of an Islamic Mosque in the immediate site of the World Trade Center disaster. This poses a new line of thought as to the real purpose of this action. The President's approval of this construction presents another question: was it considered appropriate because of the provisions of the First Amendment to the Constitution or because of the President's religion, which is Muslim.

In view of this, the founders of our Constitution had definite beliefs on what constituted protection of religion.

At the time of our Declaration of Independence, the founders based the religious structure of this country on the Christian Faith, as brought to our shores from the countries of Europe. There were different denominations of this Christian belief, and this belief was accepted and integrated into the founding of our Nation. The different denominations in their own diversity supported our Nation and Government. The Christian Faith, as implemented in the Oath of Allegiance we take, in our Pledge of Allegiance; it is printed on our currency and further displayed in many factions of our government. There were no Buddha or Shinto or other factions; there was only the Christian Faith. Many of the Founders of the Constitution certainly had European ancestors, who down through the ages over a period of three hundred years had defended the cause of Christianity by their participation in the Crusades against the Muslims.

Nowhere have I read or heard through the news media that we are faced with a Crusade for the survival of Christianity. I will leave it up to the readers of this article to form their own conclusions. My point is that I do not assume our Founders of the Constitution intended to draw up a document that would protect a religion that could or would pursue a doctrine s that would lead to the destruction of the nation they were trying to build

Is it time, based on the aforementioned assumption, that the First Amendment of the Constitution be reviewed by the highest court of this nation, the US Supreme Court? The purpose of such a review would be to decide the real intent of the First Amendment as it was originally drafted, and the beliefs and conditions that existed at the time, and to amend the Constitution accordingly.

The Muslim movement in this country is increasing every day. The ultimate goal is to destroy this country through the annihilation of the Gentiles. The moderates of the religion, who maintain this is not the case, will be run over by the radicals who are determined to destroy us. One only needs to refer to the basis of the religion. If a religious sect entered this country and believed in human sacrifice, we would rebel in an instant and abolish it. What is the true purpose of the Muslim religion, as directed at our country?

In conclusion, there is another real danger to this creeping invasion. The one area that dictates to a great deal, what transpires in the field of government, is the voters. When numbers of any group, be they Democrats, Republicans, Independents or other factions increase a voting block can develop. Deep within the Muslim Faith is embedded the Sharia Law, which dates back to Tribal Law in the seventh century; implementation of this set of laws is another of their goals.

There is no doubt that my mention of Constitutional Amendment will bring outcries from all directions. In answer to these outbursts I offer this; the Constitution is and has been the Insurance Policy of our Nation. It has persisted for over two hundred years and served the Nation well. Like all Insurance Policies, whether they are for business or personal purposes, they require reviewing and updating from time to time as to their adequacy for our protection. The Constitution requires the same attention. There have been numerous amendments for improvement to this great document, and the Nation has survived. Based on my hypothetical assumption it is now time for such action.

This writer supports any person's form of religion, as long as it supports the cause of this Great Nation. I would enjoin all readers, who would like to enlighten themselves to a bit of Sharia Law, to read Nonie Darwish's Book, "Joys of Muslim Women". I have read a few excerpts and it is very chilling. I developed my belief, that the current President's religion is Muslim on the fact he lived with his mother and stepfather in Indonesia in his early years as a boy, where it is customary to school people in the religion.

Published In the Military Officers Association
of America Magazine, November 2011

Military Pay Cuts

"A well founded military must be rewarded properly; it cannot prevail on patriotism alone". I wrote the following article. The Military Officers of America Association published it in their magazine. During the last four decades that I am personally aware of, there has been a continued effort to equate military pay to the civilian scale. This article explains why it is neither feasible nor ethical.

I retired in 1970 after 32 years of service. Two of those years, I spent with the Idaho National Guard. The remaining 30 were as a member of the Navy. Fourteen of the Navy years were as an enlisted man, the rest as a commissioned officer.

As an enlisted man, I was an engineer, and the day went as follows: I (started) with standing a watch from 0400 to 0800. Upon completion of the watch, I spent the next eight hours working in the engine room; then it was time for another four-hour watch. This adds up to 16 hours and it is still the same day. This routine goes on for a week, then the watch is dogged and there are different hours of watch standing, but the total hours involved remain the same. There was no overtime pay, no union to which to voice our complaints of working conditions, no sick leave if I became ill, and no board to review any complaints if I suffered verbal abuse. None of this was expected, and we continued to serve. As a commissioned officer, the routine was similar, but the extra hours I put in during a day's work were all part of my responsibility as an officer.

Why did I continue to serve my country for 30 years? The answer is I loved my country then as I do today. I never bucked for more pay, I simply worked hard for promotion and was happy when it happened and lived within the pay structure it produced. Retirement was something down the line that I would enjoy. It was not the factor that prompted me to continue my service.

I found this attitude prevailed with all of my shipmates. Months of deployment were accepted, and our spouses and our children carried on with their daily lives. Wives took over the responsibility of the husbands and held the family together until their return. There was no returning home after an eight-hour workday, and it was accepted. This "opportunity "is open to all who can qualify, but for some reason not all want to pursue it. I wonder why.

The last four decades have produced a continuing attempt to change military pay and retirement to a civilian base. There is no comparison between the two, nor should there be. The demands on a military service member are unique, because they cover such a broad field of requirements. This fact is missed, by most of those who would attempt to equate us differently. I am well aware of the need for the nation to adjust its expenditures, but to jeopardize its future security is unwise. A well-founded military must be rewarded properly; it cannot prevail on patriotism alone.

Published in the Coeur d' Alene, Idaho Press September 7, 2012

Voice from the Wilderness

Perhaps mine is a voice from the "Wilderness", but I feel that voice is better than no voice at all. Time is running out on the decision to change the political direction of our great Nation. Almost three years ago, I began to form an opinion on the "change" our current president introduced to the people of this nation. It is briefly outlined below in this letter. During this three-year period, I know of at least three books that have been written, by best selling authors, which have substantiated in great detail by considerable research, my thoughts. My thoughts have not been developed in a frivolous manner. My lifetime has been a witness to many challenges to our great nation, the Depression, with all of its misery, World War II with a nation unprepared to defend itself, but rising to the challenge and prevailing in its greatness to survive. This was all followed be a constant growth of our economy, industry thrived and we met all of our national challenges. Our families were presented with a lifestyle unheard of in my adolescent years. Personal integrity thrived and we worked our way to the world stage of respect and accountability to our friendly allies. Sadly, this has all been undermined by our current president's agenda and the despicable "gutter style political campaigning". There is a great deal at stake at this election, the economy, the backbone of our lifestyle, and the continued existence of our Nation as a respected member on the "World Stage". With these thoughts, I present the following analysis. I think the message has to be told frequently, until the final decision is made.

The Jury, "The Great American Voters", is out until November. They will be trying to decide if our Democratic Republic will continue to survive or go the way that all great democracies of the past have gone, once they lost their will to work and defend their government. This is probably the most decisive decision "The Jury" has been faced with in my 90-year lifetime.

To start the decision-making process "The Jury" will have to go back to 2008, when the incumbent President appeared on the political scene. They will have to decide just where and when this man appeared on the stage of politics, and what his platform for election was. They will also have to determine his character, his educational base, his political achievements, and his goal for the nation if elected. This may be a very hard task for "The Jury", for there is a great deal of missing information on the man. For a man who campaigned for total "transparency" his wall of "opaqueness" makes the "Berlin Wall" and "The Iron Curtain" look like a picket fence.

Let us begin with his patriotic base for our country. He has none and does not possess the qualities that we take for granted in a presidential candidate. Most candidates enter the Presidential Arena with a goal of building the nation. His goal has been to tear us down, apologize to the World for the actions we as a nation have taken, which in many cases has involved unilateral agreement with other nations. That simple feeling for God, Country and the Union he totally lacks. His desire to remove God from everything our Forefathers believed is evidenced almost daily. The list goes on, but he covers his tracks by issuing daily statements or Presidential proclamations that completely reverses any- thing he may have previously stated. He is a good student of human psychology. He knows we tend to remember the last thing we hear, so covering a previous statement with a new falsehood is no problem.

As a student of Constitutional Law, he has learned many ways to circumvent its requirements in order to implement his agenda, and he has an agenda. He has been described as inexperienced in the field of business, and as a leader he appears to be a sham, with no specific plan. Let this not be a true evaluation of this man's abilities, for he has an agenda and the plan is evident to anyone who will take the time to analyze what he has accomplished or attempted. Every action is a move to Marxist Socialism with an increase of government control or intervention. The result is a further decline in the economic structure of the nation and more and more control of our individual lives. By his guile, sweet-talking, and manipulating the facts to his advantage he has pulled the biggest scam on the American public in the history of our nation.

For almost four years, our nation has been wearing his mantle of "Change". No political party if they believed in our country whether Democrat or Republican should support or idly stand by and witness this slow and purposeful denigration of our nation.

Let us pray the "Jury", in its final days of deliberation, will render a verdict strong and meaningful that we will not submit to a politically motivated subversion of our country.

Please do not attempt to call me unpatriotic; I served my country for 32 years, from before Pearl Harbor, where I happened to be on that fateful day, until the "Iron Curtain" dissolved and the "Berlin Wall" lies in shambles. The supposed principals of the present administration were not the ones to which we of my time swore allegiance. Wake up America.

Published in the Coeur d' Alene, Idaho Press Dec. 12, 2013

Pearl Harbor: Don't Let Memory Fade Away

Seventy-one years seems to have diminished the importance and memory of a fateful day for our nation. The coverage of the event, although of significance to Mr. Emory mentioned on page nine of the Coeur d' Alene Press, dated Dec. 7, fails to honor those who perished and to our nation that arose to the threat and devastation of the attack.

The citizens of our great nation today do not comprehend the significance of that day, from it the nation rallied and came together as never before in the history of our country. We were jolted out of our lethargy of isolationism, and we responded as never before.

The world threat in those days of the early 40's was confined to a very small area as to what the world faces today. Throughout the world today, we, the United States, is being assailed in every quarter of the globe, and political correctness seems to want to sweep this under the rug. History, in spite of many so-called experts, does in fact repeat itself. Individual complacency can and will subject our nation to a challenge far greater than what happened at Pearl Harbor.

It is my firm belief that every paper, local as well as national should endeavor to inform and teach the uneducated what the real significance is of Dec. 7, 1941. We were unprepared and many brave and innocent men gave their lives for the mistake.

The Pearl Harbor Survivor's Association has now disbanded because of our members ages and the number that have passed on to their final anchorage, but our motto lives on and should be emblazoned on the front page of every newspaper on Dec. 7: "LEST WE FORGET; REMEMBER PEARL HARBOR".

Published in the Coeur d' Alene, Idaho Press

Culture versus Technology

It was the winter of 1937/1938 and I was attending a small high school in Hailey, Idaho. The student body was very small. There was seldom any activity outside our small realm that influenced us in any way. One day this changed and the topic of the day has stayed with me all these years.

The Principal had scheduled a guest speaker to address the student body at a general assembly, and we students were anxious to hear what the topic of presentation would be. Once assembled in the small auditorium the principal introduced the guest speaker. I do not remember the gentleman's name, but his appearance was impressive to a group of small town students. He was dressed in a grey suit, had grey hair, and a small grey moustache; to me he presented a very distinguished image. I was anxious to hear what his subject of address would be.

His opening statement invited us to understand and reconcile the ongoing conflict between Technology and Civilization or Culture, as I desire to interpret it. In my mind, civilization is the result of a nation's culture. It is important to know and remember that at this time Europe was in the process of developing under Hitler and Mussolini's domination.

Our guest speaker outlined how technology had developed over the years and centuries, and how civilization had attempted to keep abreast of technology, thus stabilizing good developments with man's ability to use it to its best potential. The point that he made was that inevitably in time, mankind fell behind and technology was misused. He emphasized that the end result was most always war. Technology was then directed to the destruction of mankind. The situation in Europe, existing at that time, was his prime example.

The speaker continued to go back in time, and to point out various moments in history that sustained his thesis, that technology and culture (civilization) tend to run parallel to one another only for a short period. The end result being that technology gets too far ahead of man' ability to use it properly. The Dark Ages was a prime example of man's degeneration to the point where the Renaissance evolved to rebuild his personal culture.

Frequently, over the years, I have reviewed this proposition in my mind. I constantly find far too many instances where this analysis prevails. One can simplify it by finding minor things such as the invention of the wheel; a great and simple invention but it did not take man long to figure he could put it on a chariot and make a war machine that could be used to his advantage to kill people.

The list is endless. Man discovered fire, which helped him cook his food. He then learned use it to raze a village or a township. Electricity lit up the world, and then we used it to electrocute convicted felons. One of the first uses of the airplane was in World

War 1 as a bomber. The list goes on; the automobile kills more people because of its misuse than any other one item. The flagrant misuse of the cell phone and the texting that goes with it. We developed the atom without developing a way to harness its destructive power. It produces power for long periods of time, but controlling it once the fuel cells are depleted we are left with what to do with a substance that still has a half-life that can be a hazard for decades. Addicts misuse our world of medicines. These medicines were discovered and developed to aid and prolong our lives. That not only destroys their lives but others as well.

It is not technology that creates the problem but the lack of culture in the human individual to handle it properly. Over the last five decades of my life, I have witnessed a constant decline in our society's ability to use properly what has been developed around us. Why is this so? The most flagrant misuse of a medium is television and its programming. At every channel there is violence or macho programs; in time this produces an impact on ones thinking and behavior. This is particularly true in a young mind. Television is one of the greatest teaching mediums we have, if used properly, and it is not. Why do I say this, because it has the basics of teaching, show and tell. The mind responds to this technique quite readily. Why do you think advertisers spend so much money researching the physiology of the human mind to sell you something you really do not want or need.

The recent tragedy of the horrible shooting in Connecticut has created a nation-wide outcry to change gun control, citing that the gun is the culprit in this terrible case. I use the comments I have made in this article to refute this approach. People, it is our culture, which is to blame. We do not pay enough attention to what is going on around us; we remain oblivious of our fellow man and fail to recognize that is where most of our problems reside. We abuse the benefits that our modern technology has given us. The next time you get in your car remember you have the potential at your fingertips to create your own tragedy. Work on your culture and become a better human being. Remember all those electronic devices and toys are great, but not when you are behind the wheel of your vehicle.

In closing, I would refute the oft-heard statement, "Oh, it is just because of the Times"; The "times" do not just happen; the social attitude and behavior of people create the "times".

Published in the Coeur d' Alene, Idaho Press April 18, 2014

Creationism and Evolution

The following comments and analysis are offered as a personal opinion that creationism and evolution should be viewed as complementary to each other. This idea is not intended to be sacrilegious in any sense of the word. This writer is a firm believer of an almighty God and Creator, but he believes there is a definite connection between the two beliefs.

Billions of years ago the first cell of life became a fact. Exactly what form or direction it would take was in the mind of the creator, but there was a plan. That cell would have to grow and adapt to a newly formed earth that was in a violent stage of development. It would have to pass through conditions unimaginable to human beings today. That cell would have to survive a consuming period of time. It would have to overcome the violent formation of earth. This would be an earth devoid of a livable temperature, no atmosphere, violent earthquakes, and an earth on which only a God given gift, life, could exist.

That cell would multiply and develop its existence to overcome these tremendous obstacles of earth's creation. It would progress through various stages as the Creator had intended, which in time would become man and woman as we are today. The Creator knew humans, as we know them today, could not exist in the conditions that prevailed at earth's birth. Thus, he willed a path of slow evolvement that in time would overcome these perils. Somewhere in that first cell, there were the ingredients that would one day become man and woman, but that evolvement would take place, over time, to adjust to the changing conditions of earth's eventual formation.

That initial cell would follow many different paths before it would one day reach the stage of being a primate. What those various stages were, may never be known, but the design our Creator, God, had in mind adjusted to each of those stages of earth's development. In time that cell reached a point where man and woman had become a full body capable of mental reasoning. With that capability they began to accept the fact there many things about them, which presented questions. They did not have an answer.

This realization of events around them, which at times may have been fearful, undoubtedly posed the question of, "why". Why did the sun rise and set, where did it go, what were the stars, why didn't the moon shine every night, why was it cold at some times, and then hot? Perhaps even the death of one of their kind imposed a fear. With all of these questions, they had to turn to some belief for answers and help. These conditions may have been the reason man and woman Created their God. Not the one we worship and believe in today, but one that might be the answer to calm their fears. It is not blasphemous to say they had their God, for this is a time eons before the formation of Christianity. It was the time of evolvement when their God passed through many phases of belief. Their God was their religion, and included times of worship to idols, sacrifice, both animal and human, elements of the universe, and Gods of self-design to fit their spiritual needs.

It is my belief that our Creator, our God, did not intend to place a completely composed and perfect man and woman on earth at one time. His design was to provide a living cell that would grow, mature and eventually evolve into a being capable of sound reasoning and positive belief in right from wrong. The many obstacles to overcome with the development of our earth were the stepping-stones of evolution.

The fields of Anthropology and Archeology have traced many of the steps in the evolvement of humankind, and there were many. To my knowledge, they cannot or have not been able to decipher the path or the full intent of that first cell of life. That answer must remain with our Creator, our God. If there is any doubt as to his intent, just look around and see the wonders he created to help ease and comfort humankind on his journey through life. The flowers and fauna, no two are alike and pay attention to the delicacy of each. The abundance of minerals he created on earth for man to develop into the many necessities we enjoy today, and the trees of beauty that provide the atmosphere that surrounds us and cleanses the air that we breathe. Most important of all is the soul he gave us as an individual being, which is a power incapable of being defined. All of this evolved from his creation. Is there any doubt that the first cell and its creation and evolution are not essential to each other?

Epilogue

An "Ode" to Himself
You have lived life's journey, whose decades past
Have given you memories that forever last,
From childhood days to old age supreme
You have lived and gained most every dream.

Life's footsteps at times have brought you pain,
But not every day has brought you rain.
In youth you struggled with a mother lost
To death, so young, a terrible cost.

But youth survives, you carry on, to find
Life's goals that must be won.
Along those paths you found the joys,
Of only things reserved for boys.

Tall mountain peaks, with shaded glens,
Rippled trout streams, with finny gems.
Long hours you spent in this paradise sweet,
But life's growth requires you must retreat.

To fend and conquer life's daily grind
By constant struggle to improve the mind.
Your childhood days at times so bright
Were often dimmed by parental fright.

Of a father loved, who, with no love to share
Could never reach to you and care.
That love you had and held so dear
Slowly washed away, replaced by fear.

The years rolled by as you slowly grew,
As a youth you traveled wide, and friends were few.
The time at last had come to leave,
A home, a school, but not to grieve

Perchance life's path was cast at me,
When I chose the navy and a calmer sea.
The storm tossed waves at home were rough,
I swore allegiance to the Navy, at home I had enough.

Thirty years you served across a world so wide,
Served your nation, served with pride.
Served in war, served in peace;
Years of absence at last would cease.

To share this tenure you had found a wife,
Who shared your love, helped build your life,
Stood by your side when times were tough,
Believed in you when goals were rough.

Gave us a daughter, so fair so fine,
She brightened our lives, a gift divine.
Her lovely smile, her love so sure,
Gripped your heart, helped you mature.

To a father proud, as proud could be,
She grew to a lady so perfectly.
Retirement years slipped slowly by,
And with each year you heaved a sigh.

For health had always ruled supreme,
You lived content within your dream.
But a static life will never last,
Good health in time will be the past.

And with the change came doubt and fear,
Your faith in God helped dry the tear.

Gave you strength, revived your soul,
To carry on became your goal.

The struggle with time to carry on,
Became a victory that must be won.
In your heart you would always know,
That life's sunlight, in time, will lose its glow.

When the last volley has been fired,
The colors folded, and retired,
Please no tears or grief display,
Just smile and say, we are happy he happened to pass our way.

THOUGHTS, MEMORIES AND OPINIONS - REVIEW

Thoughts, Memories and Opinions reflects Fred's many years of adventures and growth in his life. Those experiences have allowed him to compose a wonderful collection of poetry, short stories and insight. Fred has a very special gift for writing, which allows the reader to be involved with both the emotion and the journey involved in his writings. Fred is an inspiration to all of us. I have known Fred for several years and continue to be inspired and impressed with his encouragement for others, his integrity and strong love for his country. I thank Fred for the sacrifices he and his wife have made for our country and I know you, as a reader, will agree after reading Fred's latest book, Thoughts, Memories and Opinions.

Beverly Seaton Ingersoll
Author: 4 Months of God's Mercy